HARDY FUCHSIAS

Step by Step to Growin

George Bartlet

First published in 2000 by
The Crowood Press Ltd
Ramsbury, Marlborough
Wiltshire SN8 2HR

British Library Cataloguing-in-Publication Data

A catalogue record for this book is available from the British Library.

ISBN 1 86126 332 5

Line-drawings by Cy Baker.

Photograph previous page: Wharfdale.

Typeset and designed by
D & N Publishing
Membury Business Park, Lambourn Woodlands
Hungerford, Berkshire.

Typeface used: Plantin.

Printed and bound by Craft Print International Ltd, Singapore.

Acknowledgements
The author is extremely grateful to Roger Gilbert of Silver Dale Nurseries, North Devon, for allowing the photography of his many superb plants and for giving permission to use the descriptions contained within his extensive catalogue.

Contents

Preface

The popularity of the fuchsia continues unabated. This is quite understandable when the delicacy of the ballerina-type flowers and the vast range of colours are seen. Add to this the versatility of a plant that can be used in so many different ways. Few other garden plants can also be grown as large specimens in pots on the patio, as stately standards, soaring pillars, fans and espaliers, graceful trailing basket plants, miniature bonsai-type plants, and hedges.

Within the pages of this book an attempt has been made to encourage the reader to grow more fuchsias within the freedom of the hardy border, where they will have the opportunity to spread out their roots and reach up towards the sun, so that good, healthy foliage and vibrancy of flower colour can be displayed.

The question most frequently asked by prospective purchasers concerns the hardiness of the chosen plants. Can they be planted in the garden, left there over the winter months, and still be alive in the spring? Although some fuchsias are too tender to be planted in the open garden there are, nevertheless, many others that will safely come through the winter months and provide a first-rate annual display.

Versicolor.

A bed of hardy fuchsias.

In the spring the speed of growth of these hardy plants is nothing short of miraculous – from April onwards fresh shoots growing from a root system hidden beneath the soil are of such strength and vigour that flowers will appear on the long, arching branches by the beginning of July – a miracle indeed!

There must be a space somewhere in your garden for a hardy fuchsia – it is to be hoped that this book will encourage you to fill it.

George Bartlett.

Introduction

A hedgerow ablaze with red and purple flowers dancing in the slightest breeze creates an impression that is hard to beat. Such sights can be seen on the west coasts of England, Wales and Scotland and across the Irish Sea on the Emerald Isle.

The flower that creates this visual impact is a small, simple blossom which, because of the multitude of blooms produced, gives the impression of a burning bush. However, the flower is not a native of these isles – it originates from the southern tip of South America. There, on the Magellan Straits, the ancestors of our fuchsia hedges can be seen growing in their natural habitat.

How lucky we are that in the very early 1700s an intrepid explorer, Father Pierre Plumier, whilst hunting for plants that produce quinine, came across the first fuchsias known to the modern world. On his return to Europe he dedicated this 'new' plant to Leonard Fuchs, a botanist who lived in the sixteenth century.

The story has been told on many occasions, in many other publications, as to how these plants

A fuchsia border.

Rufus.

arrived on our shores, but I have yet to discover how plants of the *F. magellanica* strain established themselves on the western fringes of our coastlines. But establish themselves they did and have now become a part of the natural landscape.

It is from *F. magellanica* strains that the hardiness of our many modern hybrids has come. It is thanks to them that we can plant out many of the larger flowered fuchsias in our garden borders and leave them there to come safely through the winter months.

How would you define a hardy fuchsia? Perhaps it could be defined as 'a herbaceous shrub which, following severe frosts, will lose its foliage and flowers but will, the following spring, send up fresh, strong-growing branches from the root system that will be of sufficient strength to produce good foliage, buds and flowers by early July'.

I feel that any fuchsia which, in your location, can fulfil these simple criteria can be described as hardy. I have carefully inserted the words 'your location' because it is impossible to be absolutely dogmatic and state that any particular cultivar is hardy in any location. There is a great deal of variation in the amount of frost and severe weather experienced throughout these islands, even within the same locality – a cultivar that is hardy in one part of the garden may succumb to the elements in another part of the same garden, which can create quite a problem! However, the element of chance and the excitement of discovering which cultivars will grow well in the open garden, for you, is one to be savoured.

Around the country there have been many attempts to hold 'trials' for hardy fuchsias. Although of undoubted interest, I seriously doubt the value of such trials and feel that, if they are held, then the plants should be given the opportunity to prove their hardiness (in that location) by remaining *in situ* for at least three years. To move them into a new position at the end of the first or even second year appears to me to negate the purpose of the trial. Perhaps it would be wiser to suggest that potential growers should carry out personal trials using plants that have proved to be hardy in locations relatively close to their gardens as a nucleus. Within such trials it would then be possible to try out some personal favourites, not considered to be hardy by other growers, to find out their suitability to your particular situation. I am sure there would be many pleasant surprises in store!

Of greater value are the hardy collections maintained around the country by individuals and recognized by the National Council for the Conservation of Plants and Gardens. We are certainly indebted to the owners of these collections for providing an indication of those fuchsias which are worth trying and for giving us the opportunity to see them growing naturally in the garden.

This book does not contain a definitive list of fuchsias that can be guaranteed to be hardy but you will find the names of plants well worth trying. If greater guidance is required then my recommendation would be to scan the pages of the fuchsia nursery catalogues. Nurseries close to your own location will carry the names of plants that have proved themselves to be fairly hardy in your area.

I wish I could say that all you have to do to achieve success with hardy fuchsias is to plant them and then leave them to their own devices. To some extent this is true, but you will find that with a little additional effort it is possible to grow a truly impressive hardy border. I hope that sufficient advice will be given within the pages of this book to enable you to achieve that success.

CHAPTER 1

Obtaining Your Plants

SPECIALIST FUCHSIA NURSERIES

Most people acquire their first fuchsia either as a gift from a friend or by obtaining cuttings from various sources. However, if you are anxious to obtain correctly named plants, it might be advisable to purchase them from a garden centre or specialist fuchsia nursery where, in theory, you should be guaranteed to get the plants that you actually want. Unfortunately, my experience of recent years is that plants obtained at garden centres are often incorrectly named. Although the same errors could occur in specialist nurseries, the plants are usually laid out and labelled in such a way that the occurrence is less likely.

My recommendation is therefore to visit a specialist fuchsia nursery where you can select your plants personally. Look for good, healthy plants, with strong, clean growths, possibly already well branched. Height is of less importance than sturdiness.

You should make your visit early in the year (February or March would be ideal) and make sure that you have a large cardboard box or some other means of protecting your plants from the cold on your journey home.

On arrival home you will need to think about where your plants will be residing for the next few weeks. If you have a greenhouse that you can keep partially heated (or even just a heated propagator) then they will be quite comfortable.

Potting On

Depending upon the size of the pots in which the fuchsias are growing – most nurseries sell plants growing in 2½ or 3in (6 or 7cm) pots – it will be necessary to examine the root system. Bear in mind that these plants were probably rooted as

Insulate your plants.

cuttings in the previous autumn and will have already made quite a good root system. If the pots are full of roots then it will be necessary to pot them on into the next size of pot – a 3½in pot would probably be ample.

Use fresh compost for this initial potting on and try to do it with a minimum of root disturbance to each plant. The type of compost you use is not critical, any good multi-purpose compost will be suitable. It is always a good idea to add grit or perlite to open the compost and assist with drainage. Finally, ensure that the label is transferred with the plant.

Growing Fuchsias Indoors

If you do not have a greenhouse that can be heated then it is possible to continue growing these plants in your home, as long as you keep the room very cool indeed.

Make a reflecting box and place it on the window-sill with the new plants inside it. The reflecting surface of the kitchen foil will mean that the plants are surrounded with light and will therefore grow straight and not be drawn towards the light from the window. At night it might be advisable to move the box further inside the room, away from the coldness of the window.

Take care with the watering of these plants and keep a very careful eye on the soft, growing tips – it is quite amazing how greenfly seem to appear from nowhere!

(Above) *Potting on.*

Spraying is preferable to watering (initially).

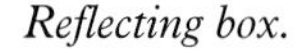

Reflecting box.

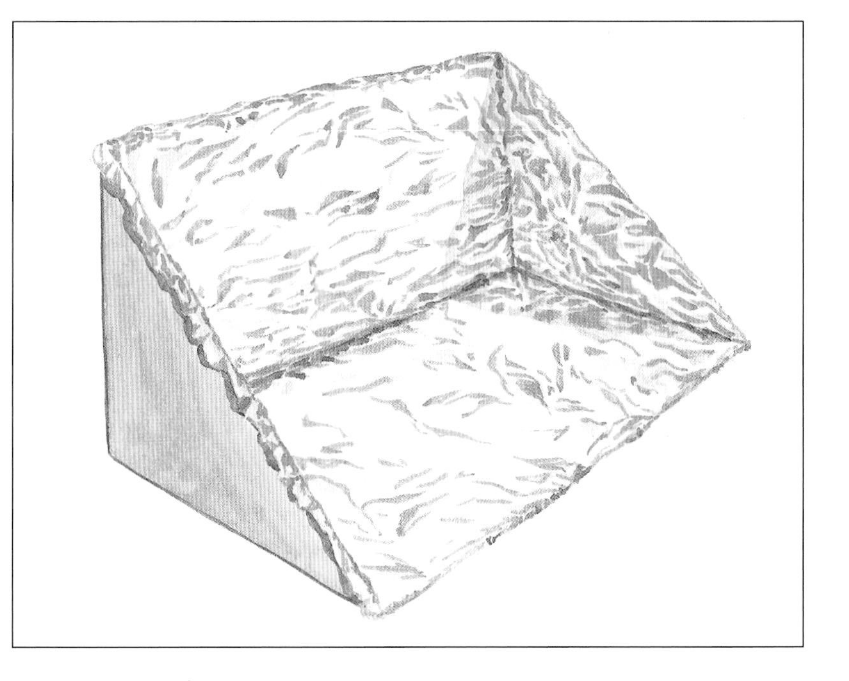

(Below) *Exmoor Gold.*

PURCHASING PLANTS BY POST

Many people do not have access to specialist fuchsia nurseries and so depend upon purchasing their plants through the post. This should not present a problem as the names and addresses of specialist nurseries appear regularly in most gardening periodicals and a fairly comprehensive list is included in this publication (*see* page 123). Order the plants early and stipulate when you would like to receive them. When they arrive, unpack them immediately. Make sure that the label is with each of the plants – nothing is more frustrating than finding labels separated from their plants.

Potting Up

To save postal charges, many nurseries send their plants with the root systems individually wrapped in moist newspaper, rather than in pots, and it will therefore be necessary to get these plants into pots as quickly as possible. The small, square 2½in (6cm) pots are ideal for this purpose and take up very little space in propagators or reflecting boxes.

Pot up each plant quickly but very carefully, making sure that the root systems are spread evenly throughout the compost. Let the compost trickle through your fingers to the root system. Do not firm the compost, just settle it by gently tapping the pot on the bench. When all the plants have been placed in their pots give them a gentle overhead watering using a fine rose on the watering can. The watering will only really wet the foliage and freshen it – the compost will already be sufficiently moist.

These plants, having suffered the trauma of a couple of days in the dark, should be kept shaded from bright sunlight until they have had the opportunity of recovering and the root system starts to continue its growth.

HORTICULTURAL SHOWS AND GARDEN CENTRES

Horticultural shows and garden centres are both popular places to buy young fuchsia plants, but I am somewhat concerned about the number of mature plants being sold in the later months of the year, the purchaser being advised by the vendor that the plants can still be planted directly in the garden.

Unfortunately, such late planting will provide little opportunity for the plants to spread their root systems deep into the surrounding soil and they will probably remain as a pot-shaped ball of roots. My recommendation would be to buy the plants but keep them in their pots and continue to enjoy the beauty of the flowers rather than planting them in the garden at this stage.

Overwintering

When frosts are threatening, the pots should be taken under cover and looked after through the winter in a frost-free place. The root system should never be allowed to dry out completely, so it will be necessary to examine each plant regularly and water if necessary. Make sure that the root system remains just moist – a dry root is likely to be a dead root.

Spring

In spring the plants can be treated in the same way as the less hardy plants – encouraged to send out fresh shoots and severely pruned to obtain strong growth from low down. It might be wise to remove the plants from their pots, tease the root system apart removing any dead or damaged roots, and repot, using fresh compost, into pots of the same size. The plants should grow strongly and can be given the protection of a cold frame until the time comes, in early summer, to place them permanently in the garden.

Whatever method you use to purchase your plants, give them a little pampering for a few days after getting them home. Make them feel welcome and they will repay you a thousandfold later.

Hardening off in a cold frame with additional protection if needed.

CHAPTER 2

Planning a Hardy Border

CHOOSING A SITE

In reality, we rarely have the opportunity to choose a site just for one type of plant. However, if we could select the best possible position for our plants, what would we be looking for?

If we think about where fuchsias grow in the wild, then we would probably assume, as they are mostly found on the tree-covered lower foothills of South America, that a type of shaded area would be the most appropriate. We know that fuchsias are not happy in full, strong sunlight and give of their best when they have relief from such conditions during part of the day. So, if we can find an area which has shading during part of the day, or dappled shade throughout, then that should be the place to use. However, there is no exact science to the growing of fuchsias – some plants, defying conventional wisdom, will grow in full sunlight without any shading whatsoever and still give a marvellous display each year. So, if you find a way that suits you and your fuchsias, even if it contradicts the recommendations made by experts, stick with it.

PLANNING THE SITE

When planning a fuchsia border or bed we must consider the size of the fully mature plants, and remember that, once planted, they will occupy the site for some years. The planning, therefore, should span a period of at least three years and the following questions must be addressed:

How big will the plants grow in the first year and will it be necessary to supplement them, to hide bare earth, with other bedding plants?

Having successfully come through the first winter, how large can we expect the plants to grow in the second year and will additional bedding plants still be required?

In the third year, how do we thin out any plants that are outgrowing the space allocated to them?

Typical Three-Year Growth

For this example I will refer to plants that I first used some three years ago. One of the plants (Genii) was growing strongly in a 5in (13cm) pot, and was well-branched with a height of about 12in (30cm) when it was placed in its permanent position. During the first season it grew fairly strongly, produced fantastic yellow foliage and was covered with flowers. It achieved a height of approximately 18in (45cm) and a spread of about the same measurement before it was eventually stopped by severe frosts in November. In the second season, new growths having come from the base of the plant during March and April, it achieved a height and spread of some 2½ft (75cm) and was a delight to behold throughout the summer. Frosts brought the display to an end just before Christmas. In the third season, the young shoots which first appeared in March but were knocked back by frosts, appeared again in April and grew to approximately 3ft (90cm) in height with a spread of some 5ft (1.5m). This plant was growing in full sun and was a marvellous spectacle through to the second week of November.

THE BORDER AND THE BED

Let us now consider two different types of presentation – the border and the bed. In each case I shall assume that fuchsias are being used entirely on their own – I will deal with the possibility of using fuchsias with other types of border plants in a later chapter.

Planning the Border

A border needs to be about 3ft (90cm) or more wide and as long as possible. Plants can be grown in lines with single specimens of any cultivars of your choice. The relative heights and possible spread of each plant is not so important, but an attempt should be made to obtain either level growth or growth which gradually increases in height from the ends towards the centre of the length of the border.

Site Preparation

The ground needs to be well prepared and we must always bear in mind that, once planted, the fuchsias will remain *in situ* for a number of years. Deep digging incorporating farmyard manure or balanced fertilizers will be of considerable benefit. It would be preferable for the digging to be completed during the autumn of the previous year.

Spring Bulbs

Spring bulbs can be used to hide the bare soil prior to the planting of the fuchsias in June. I am in favour of leaving any spring bulbs in the ground, even when the fuchsias have been planted. The foliage from daffodils acts as frost protection for the early-emerging young fuchsia shoots and the bonus of the daffodils dancing in the breeze during the colder spring months is certainly very welcome. When I prepared my border in the autumn, I positioned pots of the same size as would be eventually containing my fuchsias along the border. Then, carefully avoiding the pots, I inserted the spring bulbs. My neighbours were very amused to see me planting empty flowerpots and clearly thought I must be slightly mad! This forward planning, however, bore fruit in June when it was possible to remove the positioning flowerpots and insert the plants even though the remnants of the flowering bulbs were still in evidence. The spring bulbs were not disturbed and have provided a good display of early spring colour each year since.

Planning an Island Bed

If an island bed of hardy fuchsias is being contemplated then a greater degree of planning is necessary. Attention must be given to the heights that individual cultivars are likely to achieve. The majority of nurserymen these days include such information in their catalogues and, although this can only be a rough guide, it is useful information to have at your disposal. With an island bed it is important to have the larger growing specimens in the centre, with the smaller ones sweeping down from them to the very short ones at the edges of the bed.

Planning an island bed is a task best done during the darker months of the winter. A plan on paper can easily be amended, unlike mistakes made on the ground! To assist you in your deliberations, the fuchsias listed in this book (*see* page 51) show possible heights and spread. Again, it must be stressed that such measurements can only be a very rough guide.

An island bed.

CHAPTER 3

Planting a Hardy Border

A little extra effort spent at this stage will reap considerable future benefits as, once planted, the hardy border will be in existence for a number of years producing a good display with a minimum of attention.

Snowcap.

WHEN TO PLANT

Regardless of what part of the country you live in, the plants need to be placed in their final positions during the month of June as it is important that they should have sufficient time to establish themselves before the onset of winter.

Ideally, the planting out should be delayed until all risk of frost has passed – unfortunately, a soothsayer would be needed to forecast this for us accurately! Although there is a little risk of frost in June, it would be wise to keep an eye on the weather forecast and take precautionary steps such as covering the plants with horticultural fleece or even sheets of newspaper if the possibility of frost is mentioned. Simple 'blankets' such as these will protect the relatively tender plants from ground frosts.

Late Planting

It is not advisable to delay the planting until July or even later in the year because the most important aspect of each plant's first season is that there should be sufficient time for the root system to grow rapidly and become firmly established. Planting out in June will allow for at least four months of steady growth before the risk of early frosts in October. Delaying the planting will decrease the amount of time available for such growth.

CULTIVATION

The plants should be growing strongly in 3½in (9cm) or 5in (13cm) pots. Preferably they should be plants that started as cuttings in the autumn of the previous year. Steady growth through the winter months and

Plant deeply.

(Below) *Happy.*

careful potting on will have provided good, strong, well-branched plants with vibrant root systems.

Hardening Off

The plants should be put in a cold frame so that they harden off before being placed permanently outside. Plants given such protection during April or May will grow sturdily and can be given extra insulation from night frosts if necessary. If no cold frame is available then the young plants should be placed outside during the daylight hours only.

Frost Protection

Fuchsias are herbaceous plants that lose their leaves during the winter months and send up fresh shoots from the root system in early spring. The root system is the all-important part of the plant and must be protected at all costs. How can such protection be achieved? If we were worried about our water pipes (and a plant's internal system is not dissimilar) then we would make sure that the pipes were well insulated. The same principle applies to protecting the root system from severe frosts. The soil in which the plant is growing is the best insulation of all, and it is important to get as deep a 'blanket' of soil as possible. This can easily by achieved when the initial planting takes place. When planting other types of pot-grown plants the compost in the pot should usually be at ground level. However, I believe that fuchsias should be planted much deeper than that. If the compost in the pot is placed in a hole so that when the soil is filled in the root system is 3–4in (7–10cm) beneath the surface of the soil, then it will be very well protected.

Spacing your plants.

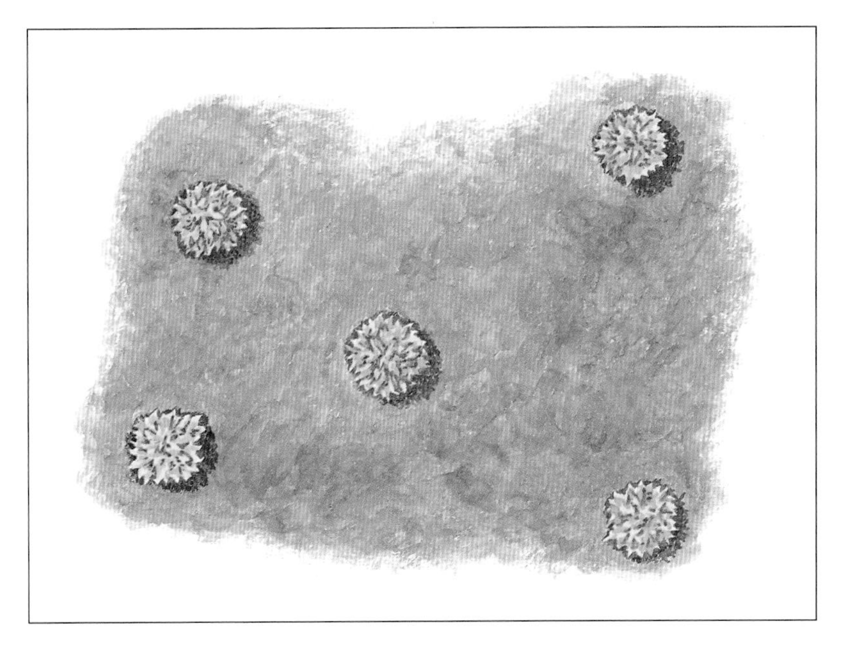

(Below) *Mr A Huggett.*

This suggestion often causes some anxiety as it would appear that a number of lower branches will be buried. However, we can be rather crafty about this and make, in the first instance, a saucer-shaped indentation in the border with the centre about 4in (10cm) deep. The plant from the pot can then be placed in the centre so that the level of the compost is level with the saucer-shaped indentation. During the course of the summer, a combination of rainfall and watering will cause the soil to fill in the indentation and the plants will sit at the correct level with their roots properly protected.

Positioning the Plants

Time spent planning the positioning of your plants will be time well spent. If you are planting a relatively narrow border of no more than 1½–2ft (45–60cm) then plants can be placed singly, in a row, each plant being about 2ft (60cm) from its neighbour. When newly planted it will look as though they are too widely spaced, but I can assure you that by the end of the first season and certainly during the second and subsequent seasons you will have no such anxieties.

With a wider border, or a large bed, it is better to plant the fuchsias in groups of three of the same

A fuchsia border.

cultivar. By this means a large splash of colour and foliage will be achieved very quickly. The plants can be positioned so that they form a triangle each 1ft (30cm) from its partner. A gap of 2–2½ft (60–75cm) should be left between each group, but even this wider distance is likely to be filled during the second season.

Interplanting

During the first season of growth, consideration can be given to interplanting the fuchsias with lower-growing bedding plants so that the bareness of the soil is not too apparent. The use of other bedding plants will give added colour and also help to protect the area around the fuchsia root systems from the direct rays of the sun.

The type of plant that you use is very much a matter of personal choice – bedding dahlias, some of the lower growing zonal pelargoniums, begonias, busy lizzy, lobelia and alyssum – in fact anything that provides plenty of colour and ground cover.

Be sure that the height of the bedding plants is not such that they overpower the fuchsias – strong foliage completely covering the whole of the fuchsia plant at ground level is our objective. Taller-growing plants in close proximity will tend to draw the fuchsia upwards and the lower foliage will be smothered and lost.

In subsequent seasons there will be less bare earth as the fuchsia plants will send up strong growths from the developed root systems.

CHAPTER 4

Care of Your Plants

THE FIRST GROWING SEASON

Without doubt the first season in your garden is the most critical of all for your plants. It is important to encourage the plants to build up a really first-class root system. This can be done by ensuring that during the first growing season no plant is ever short of moisture and a regular feeding programme is put in place.

Frost Protection

It is impossible to stress too often the need to ensure that the fuchsias are planted deeply. The natural desire of the fuchsia seems to be to send its roots towards the surface of the surrounding soil and only an initial deep planting will ensure that there is adequate insulation from severe cold for the majority of the roots. During the first season I would not recommend placing any mulching material around the base of the plants as this will encourage the roots to forage through the surface of the soil.

Watering

During this first season you will also need to ensure that the soil around the root systems remains moist so that the roots will not seek moisture from near the surface. During exceedingly hot spells it might be necessary to give a very thorough watering on a daily basis. If bedding plants are used around the relatively small plants during the first season this will provide some shading from the direct rays of the sun. Such plants also give a very quick indication if there is a need for further watering.

Fertilizers

Even though the ground would have been well prepared and fertilized prior to planting, it will help the plants to produce new growth if they are fed on a regular basis.

Nitrogen

If you look at the analysis which appears on packets of crystals or bottles of liquid feed, you will see the letters 'N', 'P' and 'K'. 'N' stands for nitrogen and is

Feed for your plants.

A fuchsia border.

the element that provides quick, succulent growth in plants. Very often you will see the recommendation that high nitrogen feeds should be given in the early part of the season to encourage rapid growth. When growing plants in pots for show purposes, such growth is necessary to produce a large plant in a short time. This is not necessary in the hardy border where short, stocky branches are much more desirable than quick, succulent growth. I prefer to use a good, balanced fertilizer when feeding hardy border plants and would not recommend the use of high nitrogen feeds such as 'Chempak no. 2'.

Phosphorus

'P' stands for phosphorus, the element that helps in the development of a good root system. An analysis that shows a fairly high percentage of 'P' is ideal for young fuchsias. If you are growing in pots, remember that rapid growth of the root system will quickly fill the pot and the plant will need to be repotted otherwise it will start to produce flowering buds. The liquid fertilizer 'Miracle Gro' is very high in phosphates and is an excellent one to use on plants growing in the hardy border or in any place where there is little or no restriction on the root development.

Potash

'K' stands for potassium, an element that is vital for the development of buds and flowers, and will also assist in the ripening process of the plant. A fertilizer that is high in potash is often recommended for use towards the end of the season when the development of buds is required or when it is necessary to ripen the wood, prior to overwintering. High potash appears to give a greater depth of colour to the flowers and foliage of many pot-grown plants. Typical fertilizers with a high potash content are 'Phostrogen', 'Vitax 103' and 'Chempak no. 4'.

The Ideal Fertilizer

So what then is the best type of fertilizer to use on border plants? We do not want quick, luscious growth and yet we want reasonably sized bushes with plenty of flowers from early in the season. A good, balanced fertilizer with equal proportions of nitrogen, phosphates and potash, such as Chempak no. 3 (20 / 20 / 20), would be ideal.

Although I have stressed the importance of watering and feeding during the first season, it should not be assumed that there will be no need for similar treatment in subsequent seasons. The best possible display of flowers can be achieved by ensuring that the root system always remains moist, and that feeding with a balanced fertilizer is continued. One of the best methods of feeding is to give a good sprinkling of slow-release fertilizer, such as 'Growmore', in early spring when the first shoots are beginning to poke their heads through the surface of the soil. The dry granules of these fertilizers can be lightly scratched into the surface of the soil around each plant.

THE FIRST WINTER

At the end of the first summer the plants will, with unrestricted root run, have grown quite considerably and should have provided an excellent show of flowers. As autumn progresses, the flowers will decrease in number and seed pods will begin to form. The removal of the pods is good for the plants as it prevents them from wasting much-needed energy in producing seeds.

With the advent of cooler, moister nights you might find that your plants, which may have started to look a little tired towards the end of summer, will take on a new lease of life and fresh, young, green shoots appear which can be used as cutting material and which, once rooted, will grow into excellent plants for using in a hardy border the following year. The method by which such cuttings can be rooted and overwintered will be dealt with in Chapter 5.

Preparation for Winter

If your plants are still providing intermittent flushes of flowers do not be tempted to remove them but enjoy them. There is little that needs to be done to the plants until a severe frost defoliates them. When this has occurred a little tidying-up operation is all that is required. Do not be tempted to remove all of the old stems that have given you good service during the summer – they will continue to work in the winter. Trim the ends back but leave the major portion of each branch on the plant as it will afford a certain amount of protection from frost to the crown of the plant. Remove any old and decaying leaves from around the base of each plant as we do not wish any diseases to overwinter. Once all the old foliage has been removed and the branches trimmed back by about a third, a good precaution would be to give the whole of the plant a good spray with a combined insecticide/fungicide. This will dispose of any lurking 'nasties' and kill off any disease-carrying spores.

Frost Protection

A mulch of bark chippings, old mushroom compost or compost from old tomato bags, can be heaped over the crown of each plant This will give the root system as much insulation as possible from hard frosts. During the course of the winter it will be necessary to examine the mulch and replace it should it be scratched away by birds.

The first winter in the life of any plant placed in the hardy border is rather traumatic – let us hope that the precautions taken in planting deeply and protecting the crown of each plant will result in successful overwintering.

EARLY SPRING

I find that from March onwards, it is usually rather exciting to examine the plants in the hardy border. The first signs of new shoots emerging from the crowns show that the plants are alive and preparing to grow strongly as the days become warmer. Do not be in too much of a hurry to remove the protective mulch blanket – severe night frosts are still likely.

Cutting Back Old Canes

You may find, especially if the winter has been relatively mild, that new shoots appear from the old canes. If you decide to leave some of the canes, remember that fuchsias only flower on wood made

Cutting back the old stems.

during the current season. Although flowers can appear from the new shoots they may be some way up the stems and it is possible that you will have long expanses of bare stems devoid of flowers.

It is far better, and stronger plants are produced over a period of time, if all the old canes are cut back to ground level when new growth is showing in abundance. By doing so you will be able to protect the young shoots more easily when night frosts are forecast, and the growth of foliage and flowers will be from ground level. I cannot overemphasize the need to pay attention to the weather forecasts – young shoots are very tender during the months of March, April and May and will probably need protection.

Care and Feeding

Plants that are growing in a bed with an underplanting of spring-flowering bulbs, such as daffodils, will get a certain amount of protection until it becomes necessary to remove the dying foliage. The opportunity can then be taken to tidy the beds. When you remove the old foliage and fuchsia canes it is very satisfying to see the strong growths coming from the root systems of the fuchsias. Once the rubbish has been cleared, you can feed the fuchsias. 'Growmore' or other types of granular fertilizers can be sprinkled around each plant and very gently scratched into the surface of the soil – fuchsias are surface rooting and it is important not to damage the 'working' roots at this stage. Following the fertilizer, a good watering will help to wash the nutrient to where it is required. It might be useful to apply a mulch around the emerging shoots to help conserve the moisture. I tend to use peat-free compost (usually composted timber and timber fines) available in most garden centres in Growbags. It is not expensive and the small amount of nutrients contained within the bags will also be beneficial to the plants.

Cutting Back Fuchsia Hedges

We will assume that the type of plant you are using to grow a fuchsia hedge is one of the strong, very hardy cultivars such as the *F. magellanica* type, so often seen in the hedgerows of Cornwall, Devon and Ireland. New shoots will frequently be produced from quite high up each stem and it will only be necessary to trim the old branches back to strong, growing shoots, keeping the shape of the plant in mind. These plants can, over a period of years, grow into quite large 'trees', so shaping and training at an early stage is important. It is also important to try to encourage fresh growths to come up from ground level so that the foliage and flowers appear from as low down as possible.

CHAPTER 5

New Plants from Old

PROPAGATION

One of the best things about growing fuchsias is that it is possible to get new plants from old very easily. Are there any secrets that will guarantee success? No, not really – as long as the plant from which you take your cutting is strong, healthy, and typical of the type of growth you expect, then success should follow.

Vegetative Reproduction

Taking a cutting is the process by which a small part of a plant is removed and given the right sort of conditions for new roots to form at the base of the stem. This is called vegetative reproduction and the young plant so obtained will take on all of the characteristics of the parent – the flowers and foliage will be reproduced exactly.

Alternative Methods of Taking Cuttings

You will probably have already noticed that there appears to be a great number of ways in which fuchsia cuttings can be taken and successfully rooted. There is no mystique to taking cuttings – whatever method you use, from placing the branches in a jam jar full of water to using a sophisticated propagator, you will probably finish up with a young, rooted fuchsia plant.

When to Take Cuttings

In order to have plants available, and of sufficient size, for planting out in June, some thought needs to be given to the time at which cuttings are taken from mature plants. Although it is possible to take cuttings at any time of year, the best time is during either September or October. This allows for nine to ten months of growth and should ensure that the plants are sufficiently mature to plant out the following summer.

When to Root the Cuttings

I have the greatest success in rooting my cuttings during the spring and autumn as I have greater

Types of cuttings from a single stem.

control of the temperature than at other times of the year. In order to root, a fuchsia cutting needs two things – moisture and warmth (but *not* heat). If a temperature of around 60°F (15°C) can be maintained, then the rooting process will proceed. During the summer months the temperature is usually too high and rooting takes much longer, if at all. Moisture is easy to supply – water.

Rooting in Water
I have already mentioned that fuchsias can be rooted in a jar of water – the only disadvantage of this traditional and popular method is that the type of root system formed is rather brittle, which often creates problems when transferring the rooted cuttings to the compost. However, such problems can be minimized by sprinkling a little of the compost into the container of water once roots have been formed. This will give the roots the opportunity to become accustomed to the bacteria in the compost. Allow about a fortnight for this process and, with luck, your cuttings will transfer to their final compost material with a minimum of trauma.

ROOTING IN AN ENCLOSED ENVIRONMENT

I have used the following method for a number of years and have found it to be very successful, simple and inexpensive.

A cutting, once detached from its parent plant, needs to be kept in a turgid state until it is able to take up moisture through its own root system. It will need to be kept in some sort of receptacle within which a high state of humidity can be maintained.

Wardian Cases

If you have read about Victorian plant growers, you will probably have come across the name of Ward who grew plants in Wardian cases. The plants were completely enclosed and the moisture in the compost and around the plants was contained within the case (growing plants in 'bottle' gardens applies the same principle). High humidity was present and the plants could live in such conditions for many months without any attention at all.

We can provide similar conditions by enclosing the plants or cuttings in receptacles such as coffee jars, large jam jars or sweet jars. The receptacle I enjoy using the most is the sweet jar as I can, within one jar, grow a strip of twelve young cuttings with virtually one hundred per cent success.

Equipment

To use this rooting method you will need the following equipment:

1. sweet jar (plastic or glass)
2. strip of twelve modules from a Plantpak (60) tray
3. compost
4. labels
5. marker
6. sharp hobby knife or scalpel
7. marking pen
8. watering can or bottle with fine rose

Compost

I use equal portions of a peat-based, multipurpose compost and vermiculite (the proportion of compost to vermiculite need not be measured out too precisely). A peat-based compost mixed with vermiculite gives a very light, fluffy compost. When I use a peat-based compost I never firm the compost, not even lightly – I let the watering do the firming for me.

PROCEDURE

The cuttings should not be kept without moisture and should be inserted as soon as they have been detached from the parent plant. So, be sure to have everything prepared – compost mixed, labels written and the module tray ready.

Keeping Unplanted Cuttings in Good Condition

If you are obtaining your cutting material from a friend and it will be some hours before you will be able to insert them, there is a very simple method of ensuring that they remain in good condition. As

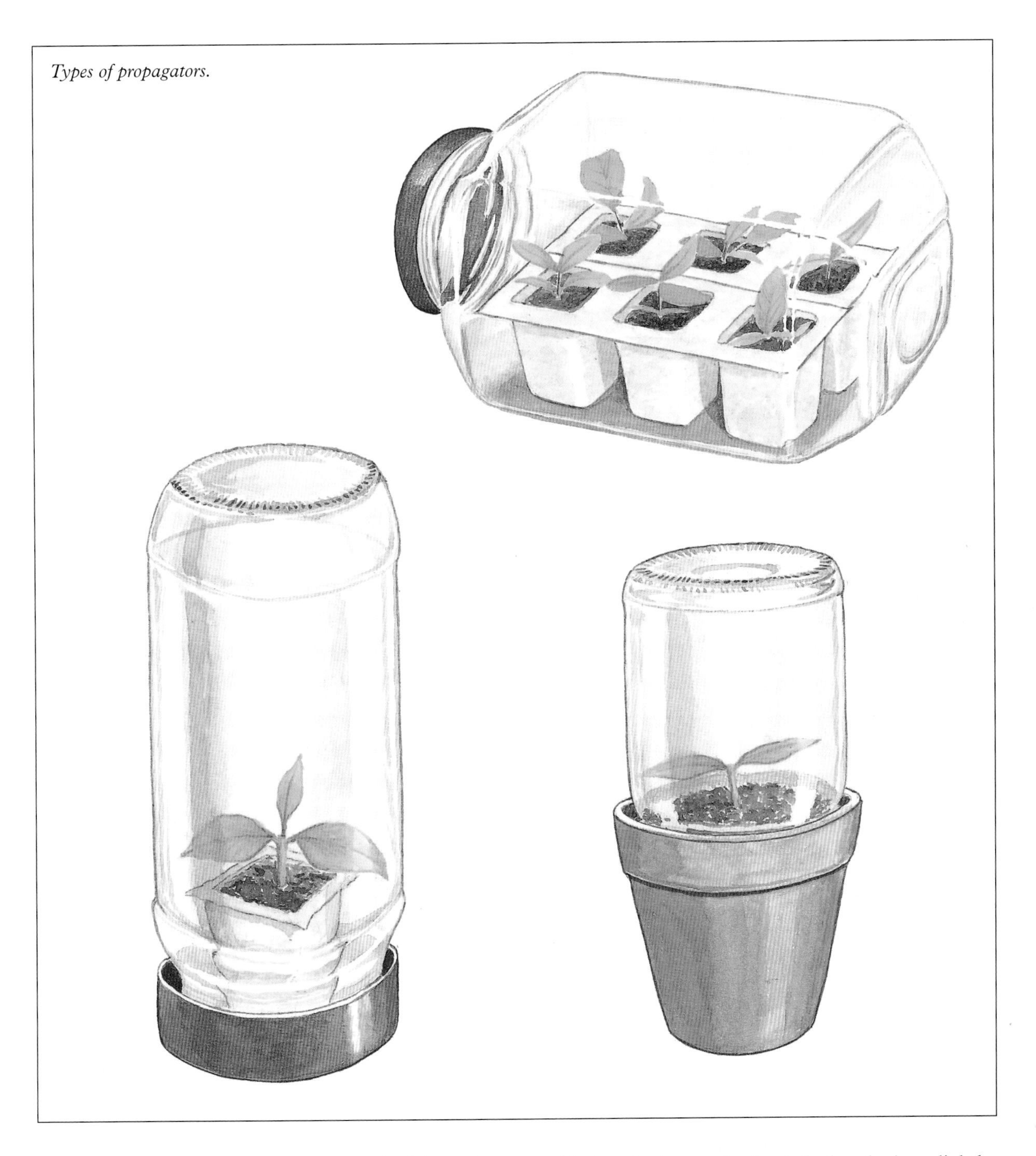
Types of propagators.

soon as a piece of plant has been detached from the parent it should have a piece of absorbent paper wound round its base, the paper moistened, and the piece (with a label giving its name) placed inside a plastic sandwich bag. A small drop of water can be added to the bag and, after inflating the bag slightly, the end should be sealed. Provided the bags are prepared in this way and are kept out of sunlight, the contents will remain turgid and in excellent condition for several hours. In fact this is an excellent

Keeping unrooted cuttings in a turgid condition.

method of sending cuttings through the post if the bags are then enclosed in a cardboard box where they will come to no harm for forty-eight hours.

Taking the Cuttings

The part of a plant that roots most easily is the soft, green tip of any branch where the hormonal activity that creates the rooting process is strongest. A perfect cutting, in my opinion, would be one that is about 1½in (4cm) in length and which has a mature pair of leaves, a semi-mature pair and the small growing tip. Remove this piece of the plant from the branch by cutting just above the next pair of leaves. It has often been recommended in the past that cuttings should be removed by cutting below the set of leaves but I have found no appreciable difference in the success rate and cutting above has the advantage of leaving the young buds in the axils of the next pair of leaves which can develop, in a few weeks, to provide more cutting material. This is not so important in the autumn, but in the spring it will form part of the process of training the plant.

Planting the Cuttings

Each prepared cutting should be gently pushed into the light and fluffy compost mixture so that the next pair of leaves is just resting on the surface. I know that some experts would consider this to be a rather unorthodox approach, but if the compost is light and airy a gentle push will cause no damage to the base of the cutting. Make a small hole with a dibber before inserting the cutting if you wish.

Filling in the gap around the base of the cutting needs to be done carefully so as not to over-firm the compost. It is important also to make sure that the base of the cutting is in contact with the compost and that there is no air gap.

Labels

The label should be inserted right away, particularly if a number of different cuttings are being taken. If you are in the habit of using 4in (10cm) labels, reduce them in size as the opening of most sweet jars is just a fraction less than that. Failure to reduce the size of the label will mean that the end cutting is flicked out of the compost as the tray is inserted into the propagator jar – annoying to say the least.

Rooting the Cuttings

When you have a complete tray of cuttings, all duly labelled, settle the compost around the cuttings by watering with a very fine rose on a watering can. The strip can then be inserted into the sweet jar and the cover of the jar screwed on. There will be no need to do any more to the cuttings until the rooting process has been completed. The sweet jar should now be placed on a north-facing window-sill or in a cool place in a greenhouse (under the benching is ideal). If no such position is available then adequate shading is of some importance as the hot rays of sunlight passing through a window and then through the propagator will create 'microwave' type conditions within the jar and 'cooked' cuttings do not root! Cuttings taken in the autumn do not need to root quickly so the coolest spot possible will be ideal for them.

You should regularly examine the enclosed propagator, but do not remove the top or worry about the condensation that forms inside the jar. The atmosphere inside, being very humid, is ideal for the rooting process. Plants have the ability to recycle the air inside the jar and do not require regular supplies of fresh air. The aim should be for a gentle misting of the inside of the propagator rather than an accumulation of water droplets which usually indicates that the propagator is in too warm a position.

After about four to five weeks the centre of each cutting will become a lighter green. You can now rest assured that the rooting process has started. There is no need to be in any hurry to remove the young plants – they can safely remain within their personal mini-climate for a few more weeks.

Potting Up

If you find that the plants are beginning to outgrow the jar then it will be necessary to remove them and pot them on into larger, individual pots. When that time comes it is advisable to wean them away gently from their perfect environment by removing the lid of the jar for a short period of time, gradually lengthening that time until the top can be completely left off.

The young rooted cuttings should be given their individual pots – 2½in (6cm) square, plastic pots are ideal. Use a mixture of three parts of ordinary peat-based, multipurpose compost to one part of perlite. The perlite will open the compost so that it is well drained but at the same time, because of its ability to absorb water, will also act as a reservoir for moisture.

Once potted individually with their labels, the young plants should be kept in as cool and as light a position as possible. Remember to turn the plants regularly so that each side will get its fair share of light and continue to keep them cool. We do not want the thin, spindly growth that often occurs during the winter months when the light intensity is low and too much heat is given. The use of a reflecting box to encourage upright growth will remove the anxiety of remembering to turn your plants.

Training

As the plants develop it will be necessary to remove the growing tip to encourage bushy growth (unless, of course, the plants are to be trained as standards). This can be done when the plant has formed two sets of leaf axils plus its growing tip. The removal of the smallest piece of growing tip is all that is necessary. When the opportunity arises in early

The first potting.

spring, place the plants out of doors but be prepared to take them under cover if the temperature falls below 40–42°F (5–6°C).

As the weeks pass, the plants should be growing sturdily and it will be necessary to continue the training process by removing the growing tips of each shoot as soon as two or three sets of leaves have developed. Keep an eye on the root system and do not hesitate to repot each plant in a larger pot if the root system develops strongly.

ROOTING IN OASIS

Another successful rooting method, as fuchsias will root readily in water, is to use blocks of Oasis. Oasis is used by flower arrangers both to ensure that their decorations are kept in place and to provide a reservoir of moisture for the branches or flowers. It has often been noticed when such decorations have been dismantled that roots have started to form on some of the branches in the Oasis.

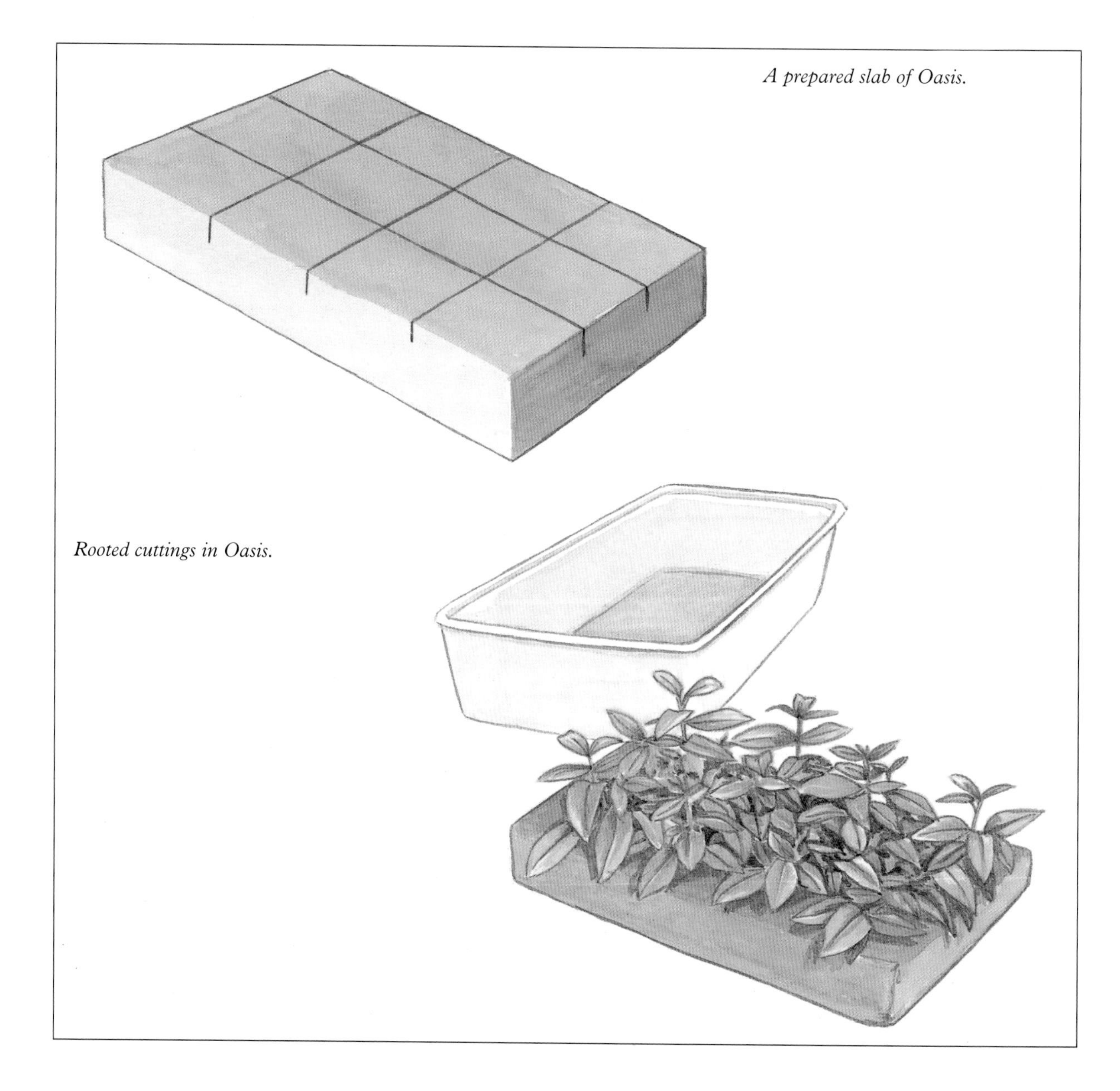

A prepared slab of Oasis.

Rooted cuttings in Oasis.

A brick of Oasis is relatively cheap to buy and can be obtained in most florists. Use a sharp knife to cut a slice of Oasis about 1in (2.5cm) thick. This slice of Oasis should be carefully scored so that the surface is divided into eight separate sections. Soak the Oasis thoroughly so that it is completely saturated and relatively soft. I find that a slice of Oasis will fit very nicely in an ice-cream or large margarine tub.

Taking the Cutting

Cuttings can be removed in the usual way by cutting just above a leaf node. However, if you take them just one set of leaves longer then you will find that the shoot will be slightly stiffer and will slip very easily into the Oasis. It is better to remove the cuttings obliquely rather than straight across the stem, and it is probably safer and less damaging to the base of the cutting if a hole is made in the Oasis with a cocktail stick or something similar.

Once the block of Oasis has been filled with the eight cuttings and the labels are in position, the container can be placed on the window-sill and left. Again, make sure that the hot sun does not come through the glass on to the cuttings as they will rapidly wilt. I find that there is no need to cover these cuttings completely as the layer of water in the base of the container will create the humidity around the cuttings that will keep them turgid. However, the complete enclosure of the container and the block of Oasis in a large plastic bag is considered by some to be an advantage as higher levels of humidity will be maintained. After about three or four weeks it will be obvious from the appearance of the cuttings that rooting has started.

Potting Up

There is no need to pot plants separately until it is possible to see a number of roots coming out through the sides of the Oasis, but you should water the cuttings with a dilute strength liquid feed (Chempak no. 3 is ideal). The plants will then get used to the type of nutrient they will be meeting when growing in a multipurpose compost.

You can pot the cuttings individually by cutting through or breaking the Oasis so that each rooted cutting is contained in its own Oasis core. If the Oasis was originally scored through to about half the depth of the block before inserting the cuttings you will find that, when breaking the Oasis into its smallest blocks, the roots slide out without damage.

Potting up a cutting grown in Oasis.

Do not attempt to remove the roots from the Oasis as this would be impossible. Pot the rooted cuttings into their individual pots by burying the core of Oasis containing the root system. Ensure that no part of the Oasis is above the surface of the compost – failure to do so will mean that the moisture will be leached out of the Oasis and the root system will suffer.

You will find that the rooted cuttings will grow away very strongly and suffer none of the delays often experienced when plants are transferred from water to a compost. Sturdy growth can be achieved by growing them on in a garden frame with the addition of overnight protection.

SPRING CUTTINGS

Although the plants will be much smaller than those grown from autumn cuttings, many people prefer to take cuttings in very early spring and the same method of taking cuttings and using a sweet jar propagator or Oasis, can be used.

Planting these smaller plants in the hardy border during June will provide less of a show of flowers in the first season and will require a little extra protection in the winter, but there is no reason why such plants should not provide excellent service for many subsequent years.

BUYING PLANTS

The easiest method of all is to purchase plants of hardy cultivars from a specialist fuchsia nursery in early spring. These plants will have been grown from autumn cuttings and your responsibilities for their development will start with the removal of growing tips to encourage bushiness. Again, these plants need to be steadily potted on into larger pots before being finally planted out in June, by which time they would be in either 3½in (9cm) or 5in (13cm) pots.

Hardwood cuttings.

HARDWOOD CUTTINGS

In the early days of fuchsia growing many of the old estate gardeners would make use of hardwood cuttings. This is a method similar to that used in rooting cuttings of privet, blackcurrants and other soft fruits. In autumn, mature 12in (30cm) stems were removed from each plant and tied in bundles. The bundles were labelled and then planted to a depth of approximately 6in (15cm) in a cold frame or a corner of the garden. In the late spring a number of sticks in each bundle had formed roots and the dormant buds along the stems were starting to break – not a very dependable way of taking cuttings but it does serve to indicate just how easy it is! A description of an experiment using this method is described later in this book (*see* page 49).

HORMONAL ROOTING POWDERS

I have made no mention of using hormonal rooting powders because I find that fuchsia cuttings root very easily without them. Although I have not found that they assist the rooting of fuchsias to any great extent they do, nevertheless, contain a fungicide which may be of use if botrytis on your young cuttings is a problem.

The only exception to this is when I am taking the hardwood cuttings in the autumn. Hormonal activity in the ripened stems will be less than is found in the soft green tips and some hormonal assistance would be useful. I prefer to use hormonal rooting liquids rather than the powders which tend to lose their viability in quite a short time following the opening of the container.

CHAPTER 6

Training – Bushes and Standards

FUCHSIA BUSHES

If you can develop a good shape during the first season in open ground, the fuchsia bush will maintain an even shape and a plentiful supply of flowers for many years to come.

Cuttings

Cuttings taken from outdoor plants the previous September or October will root very easily. They should be left to grow steadily in a reflecting box on the window-sill of a cool room. Excess heat during the winter when the light intensity is low will lead to very thin and drawn growth.

TRAINING A FUCHSIA BUSH

The initial training of a bush plant starts when the rooted cutting has formed three or four sets of leaves. By removing the small growing tip, upward

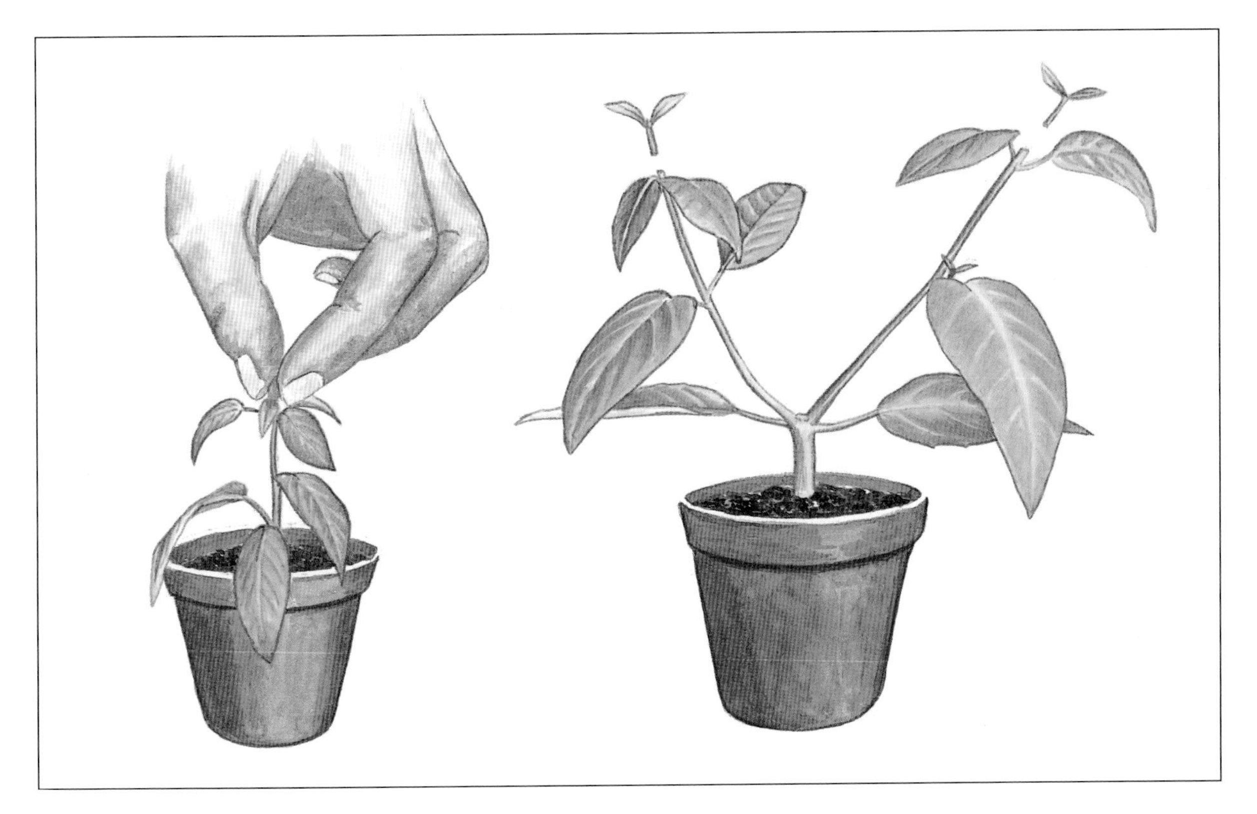

Training a bush.

A fuchsia border.

growth of the plant will be stopped and the young buds in each of the leaf axils encouraged to grow.

With three pairs of leaves on the stopped plant, there will be six young branches developing. When each of these young plants has grown two pairs of leaves and the growing tip, then the process can be repeated – taking the tip from each of the six young branches. During the cold winter months it will probably take four or five weeks to arrive at this stage. By removing these growing tips you will encourage the buds in each of the leaf axils to develop and you will have four new branches on each of the six original branches – a total of twenty-four potential flowering stems. If the cuttings were originally taken in late September they will have rooted by late October, and had their first and second stoppings in early November and mid-December respectively.

By this time, the plants may have outgrown their pots and it might be necessary to move them into larger ones. If they are growing in 2½in (6cm) pots, they could be moved into 3½in (9cm) pots. The timing of this move depends entirely upon the growth of the root system – examine it regularly and pot on if you find it is becoming overcrowded.

Maintain the steady growth in a cool room and do not be tempted to pot them on too quickly – sturdy, short-jointed plants are what is needed. By mid-January the second batch of twenty-four branches will probably have developed two pairs of leaves and their growing tips and it will be possible to remove the tips once again. Make sure that every tip is removed each time you do this – leaving just one unstopped will enable the plant to send all its strength and vigour along one branch. The removal of all the tips will give $24 \times 4 = 96$ young branches.

Repotting and Hardening Off

At the end of February or beginning of March a further potting on into larger pots with fresh compost will probably be necessary, so a final move into 5in (13cm) pots can be made. The plants will be able to stay in these pots until June when they will be placed in their permanent positions in the hardy border. Also, at this time of year, it will be possible to start the hardening off process by placing the plants in a cold frame, but be prepared to give protection from frosts if necessary. By the beginning of June the plants will have become strong, bushy specimens ideal for planting in their permanent positions.

As you can see, the training of a bush plant is very simple and basically the same as would be given to any plant that you require for pot or basket. The process of encouraging side shoots to develop by preventing any further growth along the main shoots or branches is quite natural.

STANDARD FUCHSIAS

Tall-growing standards can be used both as dot plants and to give added height to the hardy border. There is no reason why you should not grow standards from hardy fuchsias but even if the cultivars are normally good, strong plants, they must not be left in the border over the winter. A severe frost, which may not kill the root-ball of the plants, will kill the stems and it is the length of the stem that makes the plant into a standard fuchsia. You must regard standard fuchsias of any type as just temporary residents in the hardy border and be prepared to dig them up in autumn, before the first frosts.

Training a Standard Fuchsia

To train a standard fuchsia you need to encourage growth along the main stem and discourage any side growth of laterals. To this end, a cane should be placed alongside the straight stem of the rooted cuttings to remind you that the tip must not be removed. Any side-shoots that develop in the leaf axils along the stem can be gently removed by bending them at right angles to the stem so that they snap off quite cleanly. Under no circumstances should the leaves be removed from the stem. The leaves are the lungs of a plant and their existence is vital for continued upward growth. The leaves should only be removed from the stem when the standard has been completely formed with a very bushy head on top of the 'stick'.

These young 'whips', as the growing standard stems are called, can be left to grow steadily in a reflecting box on a cool window-sill. It is vital to have a straight stem so it will be necessary for the light to appear to be coming from all directions. Tie the stem very loosely to the small split cane so that there is no risk of the stem being pinched and the upward flow of sap restricted.

It is very important when growing standards to keep an eye on the development of the root system within the pot. Never allow the pot to fill with roots but pot them on into a larger pot as soon as a reasonable quantity of roots can be seen in the compost.

By the beginning of March the young whip will probably have a reached a height of approximately 2ft (60cm). At this stage you should leave any side-shoots that develop in the top set of leaf nodes. If you leave the top four sets of shoots, removing the lowest when the next set starts to grow at the top, you will have the makings of a head should any unforeseen accident occur to the growing tip and upward growth is brought to a premature end. Continue to examine the root system and increase the size of pot if necessary.

When the whip has reached the height that you require (I would suggest a total height of about 3ft/ 90cm) then the uppermost growing tip can be removed. Upward growth will now stop and the

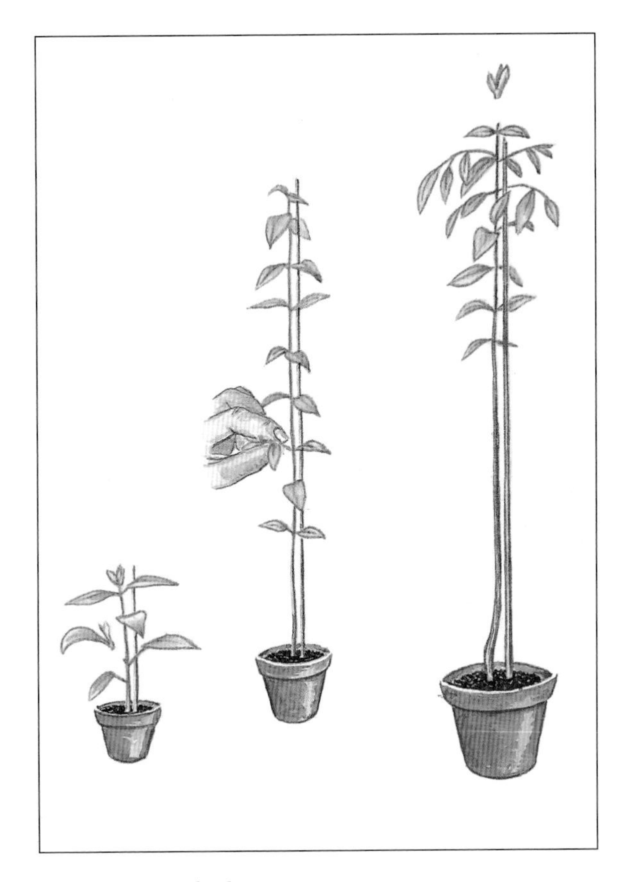

Training a standard.

(Above) *'Potting on' using a 'former' technique.*

(Left) *Standards give height to the border.*

four or five sets of side-shoots in the head of the plant will develop at a faster rate. When each of these side-shoots has two or three sets of leaves then they too should have their tips removed. This will encourage more bushiness of the head.

As the plant has been developing in height it will have been necessary to regularly replace the cane supporting the stem with a longer and stronger one. When the last stopping has taken place, a final stake should be inserted alongside the stem. This stem should be long enough to pass right through the head of the plant – later, when the standard has been planted in the hardy border, it is vital that the head of the standard should be securely fixed to this stake so that there is less risk of the head being destroyed in rough weather.

Cultivation and Care

Water

During the growing period it will be necessary to ensure that the root ball never dries out, although

Plants on a humidifying pebble tray.

it should not be allowed to stand in water. The root system needs to be able to breathe in order to grow. The air enters the compost through the drainage holes in the base of the pot. If these drainage holes are under water in, for example, a saucer, the air will be unable to enter the compost and it is possible that the root system will become waterlogged and die.

Nutrients

It will also be necessary to ensure that there are sufficient nutrients in the compost for good, strong and healthy growth. Each time you repot the plant some fresh nutrients are given, but additional feeding will be necessary within a couple of weeks. The best type of nutrient is a good balanced feed such as 'Chempak no. 3' or 'Chempak Fuchsia Food' would be ideal. The analysis on the packet or bottle of any nutrient will indicate its purpose. A balanced feed with 20 per cent nitrogen, 20 per cent phosphates and 20 per cent potash (usually appearing as 20/20/20 on the packet) will provide all that is required for good, steady growth.

During the first summer in the hardy border the plant will repay all the effort that you have lavished upon it during the winter months as long as you can continue to ensure that there is a plentiful supply of water and nutrients for the root system.

Overwintering

In autumn each plant should be carefully dug out of the border and the root ball placed in a pot of convenient size. The head of the plant should be trimmed back to about half of the length of the branch. It is advisable to remove all of the foliage and spray the completely denuded head with a combined insecticide/fungicide to get rid of any pests and diseases. If this is done during October then fresh young growths will start to appear on the pruned branches and it is these fresh growths that you need to keep 'ticking over' for the winter. Keeping plants in green leaf removes any anxiety about even breaking of new shoots on heads of plants allowed to have a period of semi-dormancy.

To overwinter a standard it is necessary to keep it in a frost-free situation and ensure that the root system is never allowed to dry out completely. Most growers prefer to keep their standards in green leaf throughout the winter – just ticking over but not really growing. To do this you need to have access to a greenhouse or outbuilding that can be thermostatically maintained at about 40–45°F (4–6°C).

Frost Protection

There are three parts to a standard fuchsia that need to be protected from the frost:

1. The root system – the pot can be swathed in an insulating material, such as bubble film, so that frost cannot enter through the sides.
2. The stem – insulating the stem by using tubes of pipe-lagging is very effective.
3. The head – wrapping the head in horticultural fleece will protect it from several degrees of frost.

Pruning

In spring it will be necessary, even if the head is still in full green leaf, to prune the upper branches further. As fuchsias only produce flowers on wood that has been made during the current season, all of the branches in the head can be cut back to leave two or three nodes on each branch. This will ensure short-jointed growth and plenty of new, young growths from which you will get the first flush of flowers.

Replanting

When all risk of frost has passed, the standards can once again be planted into the hardy border. I would always recommend removing the plants from their pots as this will reduce the amount of care that will need to be given to them during the summer. Provide a very strong stake which will need to pass right through the head of the plant. Secure as many of the branches in the head to the stake as possible so that movement of the head is minimized. Continue with the programme of watering and feeding so that good strong growth and continuity of flowering is achieved. If you decide to leave the plants in their pots, perhaps for stability, then it will be necessary, on a daily basis, to ensure that the plant is receiving sufficient quantities of water. To assist with the drainage of the compost, and also to give added weight, it might be advisable to place a layer of gravel in the hole before burying the pot.

Growing standards and using them in this way is extremely satisfying. It is also possible to buy ready-made standards (at some considerable cost) at garden centres and nurseries, but you will derive much more satisfaction from growing your own.

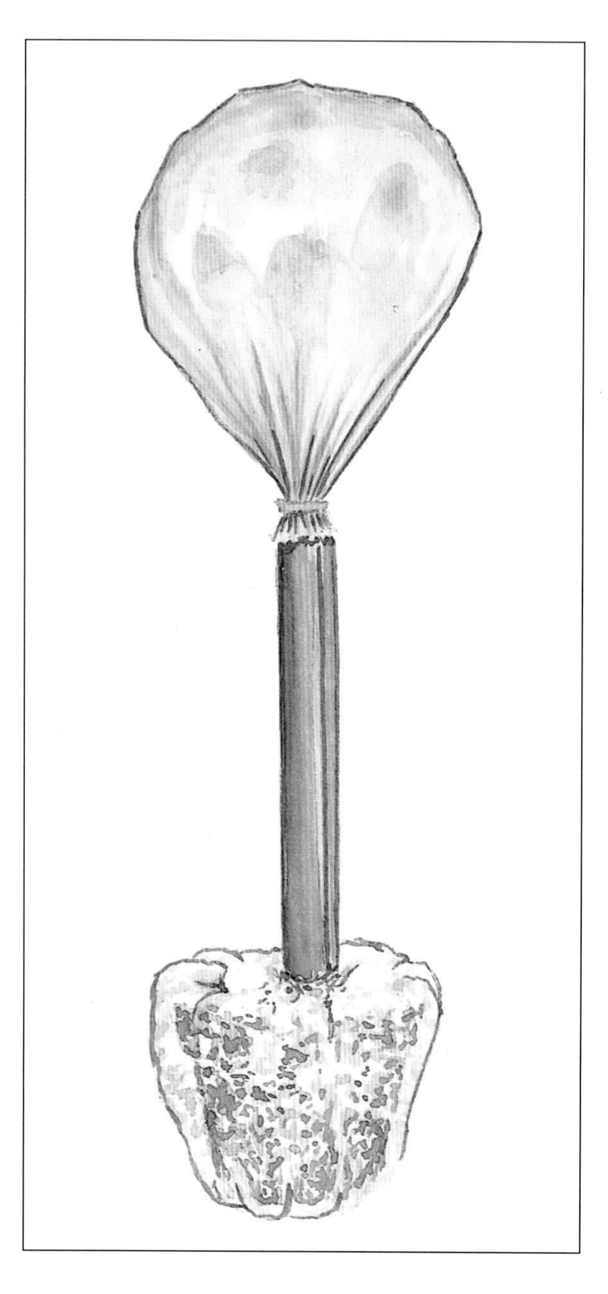

A standard ready for winter.

CHAPTER 7

Fuchsias on the Patio

POTS OF FUCHSIAS

Not everyone is lucky enough to have a garden in which fuchsias can be planted permanently. Many enthusiasts depend upon plants growing in tubs, pots or hanging containers, and some fantastic displays can be provided under such conditions.

Hardiness

When growing plants on the patio, there is no need to concentrate on those cultivars or species which are known to be hardy and able to grow permanently out of doors, with a minimum of protection. Some of the half-hardy or even tender cultivars may be used as you will will need to move the containers under cover at the end of the flowering season, before the severe frosts set in.

Frost Protection

It is necessary to move the containers because the root systems would be attacked by frost from all sides, not just the top, and it is possible that the compost contained within the pots would become frozen solid.

Pot fuchsias on the patio.

Flat Jack of Lancashire.

If no position is available for storing the resting plants under cover during the winter, you could try to protect individual pots by wrapping them in insulating material such as the felt used in attics – a practical but not a very attractive proposition for the patio.

CONTAINERS

Growing plants in containers will restrict the amount of room available to the root systems, so it is wise to buy the largest containers that you can possibly handle, bearing in mind that they will become heavier and more unwieldy when filled with compost and a large plant. Use your imagination when choosing a container – there is no need to depend upon the ubiquitous, large, terracotta-coloured pots. In a way, half the beauty of a patio display lies in the shapes and colours of the receptacles you choose.

COMPOST

I suggest you use one of the peat-based, multipurpose composts with additional perlite – such a compost would not add too much weight to the pot. A slow-release fertilizer such as 'Osmocote' or 'Season Long' added to the compost will ensure that it remains in good condition throughout the summer, although additional feeding will need to take place in order to provide a continuous display of flowers.

PLANTING AND GROWING FUCHSIAS IN CONTAINERS

Autumn cuttings are ideal for use on the patio. When planting the containers, use not just one but three plants of the same cultivar. Plant them fairly closely together so that the branches will rapidly start to intertwine and give the appearance of being just one plant. This method is widely used by specialist growers when they need to obtain large plants fairly quickly for shows and exhibitions.

It is wise to plant up the containers as early in the season as possible so that the roots will have the opportunity of growing quickly through the compost, but you will need to be vigilant and take the necessary preventative measures if frost is forecast.

Once the plants are growing rapidly, supporting canes should be inserted between them. Garden twine can be used to keep the branches upright. If the plants were growing strongly in 3½ or 5in (9 or 13cm) pots prior to planting, the chances are that they will have been stopped on a couple of occasions and will be producing a number of branches. No further stopping will be necessary and the plants can be allowed to develop, upwards and outwards, so that flowers will be produced as early as possible.

Interplanting

Fuchsias can be enhanced by, and will enhance, other low-growing bedding plants positioned around the edges of the containers. Busy lizzy, lobelia, bedding begonias, alyssum, nemesia and many others will give added colour to your patio display. It is important for the general appearance of the whole container that hard edges should be softened by trailing plants – trailing fuchsias, cascading gracefully over the edge of the pot, are ideal for this purpose.

Standards in Tubs

Additional height and variation can be given to your patio display by using plants trained as standards. If the plants are being grown for your own satisfaction, and not for exhibition in shows, there is no need to worry about the measurements laid down for the various standards, nor the size of the container in which they are grown, but try to get a good balance between the height and spread of the fuchsias and the size of the pot. The bare compost at the base of the standard fuchsia can be covered with some bedding plants or some of the lower-growing fuchsias, either bush or trailing.

Fans, Pillars and Espaliers

Other possibilities for use on the patio include some of the more unusual methods of training. A good-sized fan of fuchsia placed against a south-facing wall is a marvellous sight. Height can be obtained by growing pillars, and width by training an espalier.

(Above) *Standard in container.*

Fuchsias on the patio.

(Above) *Hanging baskets with fuchsias.*

Baskets

One of the best ways of viewing a fuchsia is to look up into the flower – the beauty of the differentiation of colouring between the sepals and the petals in the corolla can only be fully appreciated when viewed from below. Baskets or half- (or wall) baskets are ideal for this purpose. I would again recommend that a number of plants, all of the same cultivar, should be used. This will produce a good, full display of flowers – uneven flowering very often occurs if you mix the cultivars.

Troughs

If you have a window-sill or a wall upon which a trough can be placed, then you have a further place on which to grow fuchsias. The smaller-flowered, trailing fuchsias or even the rather laxer-growing, ornamental-leaved cultivars look fantastic if allowed to cascade over the edge of a trough. Dwarf-growing fuchsias such as the 'Thumb' family would make ideal plants for growing in troughs.

The ways in which you can use fuchsias on balconies or patios are legion. Let your imagination run wild – *en masse* they will always give you a fantastic show.

A window trough.

CHAPTER 8

Large Structures in the Open Garden

FANS, ESPALIERS AND PILLARS

The strength and the vigour of many hardy fuchsias make them eminently suitable for training into some of the larger structures. If you are lucky enough to have a large greenhouse where the fuchsias could be planted directly and permanently in the border, it is quite possible to grow plants to an immense size. Very few of us have such facilities, but it is possible, nevertheless, to grow larger structures if the plants are given a certain amount of winter protection.

FANS

A fan is a large bush that has been trained in a flat way, as opposed to the usual round shape, and the branches have been so arranged that the fan shape is produced. The sight of a fan-shaped fuchsia against a sunny wall is an absolute delight.

Training

An autumn cutting would be a useful starting point for a project that takes several years to reach its full potential. The cutting can be grown on a window-sill in a reflecting box and should be allowed to develop six sets of leaves before the growing tip is removed. It is important to select a young plant where the leaves are growing in pairs and in a cruciform pattern (that is, the first pair go north and south, the second east and west, the third returning to north and south, and so on). If six sets of leaves are present on the plant, the removal of each alternate pair will leave three pairs with the young branches all growing along the same plane, in the same two directions.

Removal of the small growing tip will encourage the growth of the three pairs of leaves and the plant can be given more room for the roots to develop by moving it into a 5in (13cm) pot. The first framework should be inserted so that the branches can be trained into the positions that they will finally occupy. The framework at this stage will consist of two flower sticks about 2ft (60cm) in length, pushed into the compost down the sides of the pot so that the young shoots are pointing in their direction. Further canes of the same length can be placed between the edges of the pot and the plant so that shoots can be trained along their lengths. Three further split canes of the same length can then be placed, horizontally, between the four upright canes and tied to them. As the side shoots develop they can be tied to these canes to give the pleasing fan shape.

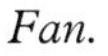

Fan.

Throughout the training process an attempt must be made to balance the upward with the sideways growth. Stopping the upward-growing shoots will encourage the growth of the laterals and vice versa.

By the end of the first year the plant will be growing strongly in a 7–8in (18–20cm) pot. It is best to overwinter the plants in a frostproof greenhouse – if it is possible to maintain a temperature of around 40°F (4°C) the plants can be kept in green leaf.

Permanent Planting in the Open Garden

During the second season you may decide to be brave and experiment by planting the fan permanently in the garden, in which case it will be necessary to prepare a piece of ground adjacent to a south-facing wall. The addition of well-rotted manure together with copious supplies of grit to assist with drainage would be advantageous. The framework of the fan should be secured to a similar framework attached to the wall and all subsequent growth trained to the new structure.

Regular watering and feeding will encourage good, strong growth and a plentiful supply of flowers throughout the whole of the season.

Frost Protection

At the end of the season when the threat of frosts becomes imminent, a decision will need to be made about whether the fan should be left in position in the garden or laboriously dug up, trimmed back, and removed once again to the safety of the greenhouse.

If left unprotected, the upper structure of the fan will usually be killed following the first severe frost, although if the plant you are using is one of the really strong, hardy cultivars then, in a mild area with few really deep-penetrating frosts, it may possibly come through the winter safely. However, I strongly recommend that you devise some means of protecting the fan.

You could follow the example of those gardeners who have fan-trained peach trees, and design some sort of framework with layers of horticultural fleece to give protection. Even one layer of fleece can give a few degrees of frost protection, so multiple layers will have an even greater beneficial effect. It will be necessary to pay careful attention to the forecast temperatures and be prepared to add extra layers of fleece or other protective material if necessary.

A hardy border.

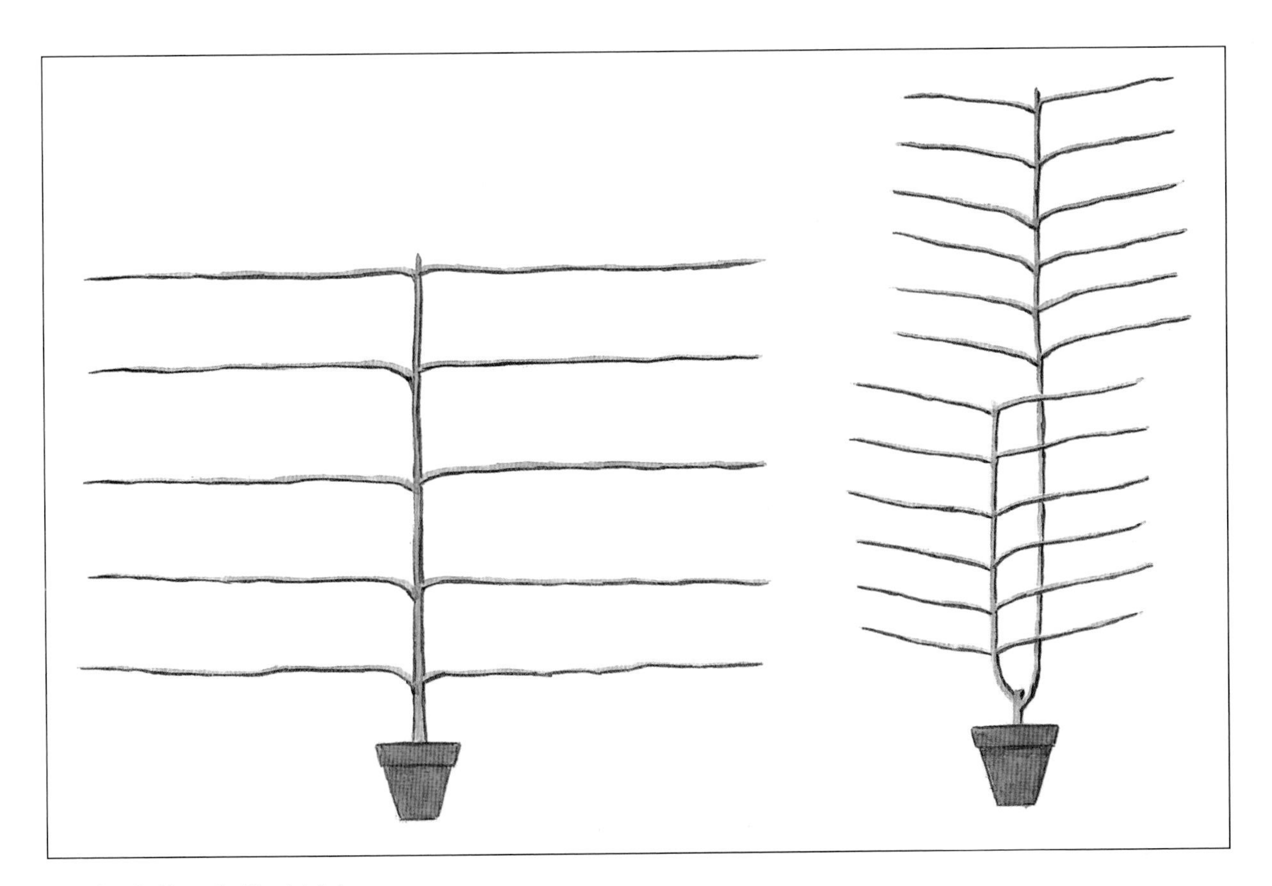

Espalier (left) *and pillar* (right).

ESPALIERS

The training of espalier fuchsias follows a very similar pattern to that of a fan with the exception that the sideshoots are trained horizontally and at right angles to the main stem. An effort should be made to encourage flatness of growth by tying in the sideshoots, and also to encourage upward growth from the horizontal branches so that the whole structure is filled with foliage and flowers.

It might be possible with this type of growth to make use of a wall as previously described and risk overwintering the plants *in situ*.

PILLARS

Many of the stronger growing hardy fuchsias are very suitable for use when growing tall pillars. Again this is a method that will take several seasons to reach full potential.

Encouragement of strong, upward growth and restricting lateral development will be necessary to achieve good heights. Ensure, especially during the first year of growing, that the plant never completely fills the pot with roots. If it does so, it will feel threatened. A threatened plant will obey the call of nature and start to produce flower buds and flowers in order that seed can be developed. We want strong, vegetative growth at the expense of flowering during this first season, so feeding and repotting will always be a priority.

Again, it is probably wiser to keep plants 'ticking over' during the winter months in green leaf. A temperature in the region of 40°F (4°C) will keep the plants free from danger.

HARDY FUCHSIAS SUITABLE FOR TRAINING INTO LARGE STRUCTURES

The following list is subjective and not intended to be definitive, others will undoubtedly come to mind.

Achievement
Alison Sweetman
Army Nurse
Baby Blue Eyes
Barbara
Blue Bush
Corallina
Display
Dorothy
Dr Foster
Edith
Empress of Prussia
Graf Witte
F. hatschbachii
Hawkshead
Lady Boothby
Lechlade Magician
Logan Woods
Madame Cornelissen
F. magellanica – (and any of the variations)
Margaret
Mrs Popple
Phyllis
Remembrance
Wharfdale
Whiteknight's Pearl

(Above) *Lady Boothby;* (below left) *Edith;* (below) *Empress of Prussia.*

CHAPTER 9

Fuchsia Hedges

Visitors to Devon and Cornwall, the west coast of Scotland, and Ireland will undoubtedly have marvelled at the beauty of the fuchsias growing strongly in the hedgerows. The sight of the long, arching branches and the delightful, though small, flowers hanging gracefully and pendulously from them is unforgettable.

Although more likely to flourish in those parts of the country with mild winters, fuchsia hedges can be grown in many other areas. If you are prepared to accept that during the majority of winters you are likely to lose the top growths of the plants, and can wait until late spring for the new growths, there is no reason why you should not have a fuchsia hedge.

PLANTING A FUCHSIA HEDGE

Which Plant?

You should choose plants which are strong enough, even when killed to ground level during the winter,

A hardy fuchsia at Borde Hill, Sussex.

to grow sufficiently strongly for flowering branches of reasonable height to be produced fairly quickly. The choice of plants is quite wide and can be taken from those listed at the end of the previous chapter (*see* page 42).

What Site?

In order to gain some protection from severe frosts it is a good idea to plant the hedge alongside a low wall. This will give shelter from any seering, icy winds and help to protect the root system.

Preparing the Ground

Thorough preparation of the ground is necessary during the autumn prior to planting when you should mix copious supplies of well-rotted manure into quite deep trenches. As drainage is a vital factor for the successful growing of fuchsia hedges, the addition of grit will be very beneficial.

Planting

Planting should take place as soon as all risk of frost has passed. If fuchsias alone are forming the hedge it is advisable to have plants of the same cultivar in a block, with each plant approximately 9in (23cm) from its neighbour. If you feel that a hedge consisting of just one cultivar is a little dull then you could plant a second block of another cultivar as long as you choose two varieties that will reach approximately the same height.

Cultivation

The first season is vital for the development of the hedge. The plants must be frequently watered and fed to ensure strong growth and the development of a good, deep root system. The first winter will be a worry, but precautions can be taken to protect the root system and it might even be possible to protect the top of the hedge from the severest of frosts by the judicious use of horticultural fleece.

However, even if the top growths are completely cut down by the frost, the new, developing stems will be of such strength and vigour that flowers will be produced by the beginning of July.

A hardy fuchsia at Borde Hill, Sussex.

Interplanting

Interplanting fuchsias with other types of hedging plants can make a very interesting hedge. A group of three fuchsias protected on each side by another hedging plant such as privet, holly or beech would safely come through all but the severest of winters. The overall length of the hedge will decide the number of blocks of fuchsias that will be required. Hedging plants with interesting colours in the foliage could make for an exciting combination.

CHAPTER 10

Pests and Diseases

PESTS

I wish I could say that fuchsias growing in a hardy border are not affected by any pests – unfortunately, they are prone to attack by a number of sap-sucking insects which can do considerable damage to the plants by causing 'blindness' and delaying the production of flowering shoots.

Whitefly.

Whitefly

Fortunately, plants growing in the open garden are afflicted rather less by whitefly than their more tender compatriots growing under glass. However, there are certain stages in the development of the plants when you need to be vigilant. Young, rooted cuttings growing steadily on window-sills are particularly prone to attack. Regular handling and inspection of the underside of the foliage will be necessary. In the early stages, rubbing out the pest using finger and thumb will rapidly prevent an infestation. When the mature plants have been placed in the border there will be less need for close inspections although it is important always to be aware of the possibility of attack.

I do not particularly like using chemical insecticides and prefer to use a soft soap solution in the initial stages of attack. There are occasions, however, when they become necessary. Plants growing on window-sills can be treated by watering a systemic insecticide into the compost. Any sap-sucking insects will be killed and no damage done to surrounding furnishings.

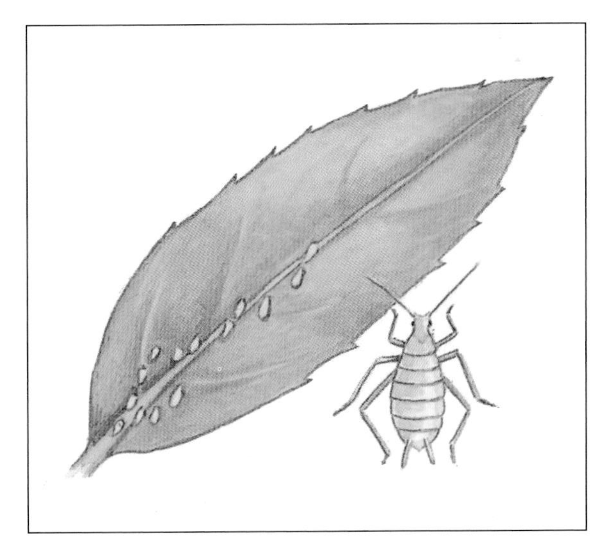

Greenfly.

Greenfly

Greenfly is another sap-sucking pest that seems to thrive in the dry conditions found in most homes.

A fuchsia border.

Prosperity.

Plants growing on window-sills are frequently attacked by greenfly causing considerable damage to the soft, developing tips of the shoots. Early discovery is necessary to prevent a severe infestation. The use of a soft soap solution, particularly if it is possible to completely immerse the top growth, is a perfect answer. Again, being sap-sucking insects, they can be effectively killed using a systemic insecticide, watered into the compost.

Greenfly are also a problem on older plants in the garden and every effort should be made to keep any infestation under control. As there are natural predators in the garden that will come to your assistance, you may only need to use a non-toxic spray (soft soap or even pure water) to dislodge the pests.

Capsid Bugs

Outdoor plants, especially those growing in fairly close proximity to trees, are often attacked by small sap-sucking insects that nibble away at the soft growing tips causing distortion and sometimes blinding of the shoots. Capsid bugs can be kept under control by using a non-toxic spray on a regular basis. A systemic insecticide watered into the ground surrounding the plants can also give some protection.

Frog Hoppers

This sap-sucker is found where 'cuckoo spit' is observed on the leaf axils of the plants. Within the froth you will find the larvae (like little green frogs) which happily nibble away at the plants. They cause rather less damage than other pests as they are rarely present in great numbers, but they can be a bit of an eyesore. A fairly sharp spray of water from a hose or spraygun will wash away the 'froth' and dislodge the insect.

Thrips

These are very small, brown or black insects that feed in large numbers on leaves and flowers. The presence of silvery specks and streaks on the leaves and flowers usually indicates an infestation. Some leaves can be very badly affected as the upper surface is removed causing a 'window-like' appearance. Damage is also done to flowers and buds, causing some distortion. Use both contact and systemic sprays when the presence of thrips is noticed. The treatment needs to be carried out at eight- to ten-day intervals.

Vine Weevil.

(Below) *A fuchsia border.*

Vine Weevils

Vine weevils are quite a recent phenomenon and fortunately not such a problem with outdoor fuchsias. As the root systems are bigger and more free-ranging than plants growing in pots, less damage will be done providing there are just a few larvae present. If the tell-tale notches are seen on the edges of the leaves, then it is possible that adult vine weevils have been at work. Watering the ground surrounding the root system with a solution of 'Armillatox' (1/250 dilution rate) will render any eggs that have been laid by the adult vine weevils sterile.

Caterpillars

Caterpillar damage is not usually a great problem with fuchsias although there is one that can create a great deal of damage in a very short space of time. This creature is the caterpillar of the Elephant Hawk Moth. It is quite alarming when first seen as it grows to about 3in (8cm) in length and has a pair of imitation eyes near the front of its brownish body. Although quite harmless to humans, it can defoliate a fuchsia plant in a very short time. When found, 'hand picking' is the only real answer.

A fuchsia border.

Bees and Wasps

Wasps spoil fuchsia flowers by biting holes in the tube and by biting off the stamens, styles and petals in an attempt to reach the nectar. Both wasps and bees cause bruising on the petals whilst carrying out this natural activity.

DISEASES

Fuchsias growing permanently in the open garden are far less affected by diseases than their more tender cousins growing in greenhouses. However, certain diseases can be brought when purchasing plants from garden centres or even specialist fuchsia nurseries.

Rust

There is no mistaking this most debilitating disease – brownish spots appear on the upper surface of leaves and copper-coloured pustules that look exactly like rust can be seen on the underside. The pustules are the spores of the disease and are very easily transmitted from one plant to another both by handling and the movement of air. If left unchecked the plants will be very unsightly and will eventually become completely defoliated.

Not so many years ago, it was considered that the only cure for rust was to remove and destroy any plant that was even slightly infected. Fortunately, such drastic action is no longer considered necessary. However, treatment is not easy and requires the careful removal of all the infected leaves, which should be sealed in bags and disposed of with the domestic rubbish. After removing the infected leaves, the plant and its neighbours need to be sprayed with a good fungicide such as Nimrod T as a preventative measure. There are sprays available that can be used to kill the spores on infected foliage but this is not generally available to the amateur grower.

Botrytis

Another disease that affects plants growing in confined spaces more than those growing in the open garden is botrytis (grey mould), a grey, furry growth found on flowers, leaves and shoots in severe cases, usually caused by lack of ventilation. It is most likely to affect outdoor plants when, during spells of damp weather, dead leaves fall across other branches encouraging the formation of botrytis spores.

Treatment consists of cutting back to good, clean wood and, especially in confined spaces, creating a more buoyant atmosphere with plenty of air movement through the branches of the plants.

M. Comber.

CHAPTER 11

Ripe Wood Cuttings

Whilst reading through some very old fuchsia books, I came across the method of taking hardwood cuttings used by Victorian gardeners. Bunches of bare twigs would be planted in a cold frame in the autumn. By the time they were removed the following spring or summer, a root system would have formed. (These 'cold frames' were something of a misnomer as most were wooden, box-like structures standing on old 'hot beds' (manure heaps), that provided a source of warmth throughout the winter.)

It is doubtful if plants produced by this method would ever make particularly good bushes, but it is possible that the young shoots developing on the stems could be used as soft-tip cutting material in the early spring. In order to ascertain whether such a method is either feasible or of any great use, I set up a series of experiments.

OCTOBER 1996

Cutting material was obtained from the following:

F. paniculata (a non-hardy species that grows strongly and produces new shoots quite readily when severely pruned back in the autumn)
F. Margaret Brown (S) (hardy)
F. Rufus (S) (hardy)
F. Genii (S and foliage) (hardy)
F. Dollar Princess (D) (hardy)
F. Garden News (D) (hardy)

Three branches from each of the cultivars, all but one being generally regarded as hardy, were removed at ground level. All foliage was removed and two pieces of stem approximately 8–9in (21–23cm) were obtained from each branch. Care was taken to ensure that the bottom end of each twig could be easily identified. Six methods of preparing the twigs were used on each cultivar:

1. Plain cutting – no treatment.
2. Plain cutting – end 'stippled' (the bark at the base of the cutting is tapped with a sharp blade to cut through the surface of the skin).
3. Cutting dipped in hormonal rooting powder.
4. Cutting stippled and dipped in hormonal rooting powder.
5. Cutting dipped in hormonal rooting liquid.
6. Cutting stippled and dipped in hormonal liquid.

Each cultivar was given its own 3½in (9cm) pot filled with a mixture of 50 per cent peat-based multipurpose compost and 50 per cent vermiculite. Labels were attached to indicate the type of treatment received and the six cuttings were inserted, using a dibber, into their designated pots.

Garden News.

When all the pots were filled, the whole tray was given a thorough watering using a fine rose on a watering can and placed on the top shelf of a greenhouse which was kept at 40°F (4°C) throughout the winter months. The tray was examined regularly to ensure that the compost did not dry out. If young shoots started to form on the twigs, damage by aphids was prevented by spraying with an insecticide.

Five months later, in early March, it was possible to see some results.

The experiment proved to have been very successful. All of the cuttings taken, with the exception of a few of the *paniculata*, rooted well and produced an excellent supply of young material that could be used as early spring cuttings. This growth was produced during late and early March, long before any growth was shown from the bases of the plants in the garden.

Although most of the young growth came from the upper parts of the cuttings, sufficient branches formed lower down for the cuttings to be planted in fairly deep pots with the majority of the stems beneath the surface of the compost. These pots eventually produced superb plants for the patio.

The only surprise was that the type of treatment received prior to planting appeared to have made so little impact on the plants. Nevertheless, I would still recommend using a hormonal rooting powder or liquid for hardwood cuttings even though no great improvement in performance was noted.

OCTOBER 1997

In view of the success of the previous year's experiment I decided to use the same method for obtaining young cutting material in early spring.

There had been some early hard frosts and, whereas in the previous autumn the sticks had been removed from the parent plants prior to natural leaf fall, on this occasion the plants had been denuded of their leaves by the severe frosts.

The same methods were used to treat the twigs (except, of course, that defoliation was not necessary), and the winter treatment in a cool greenhouse was the same as previously described.

The results on this occasion were completely negative – none of the cuttings rooted. The severe frost had not only defoliated the plants but had also killed the stems. Therefore in future years it will be necessary to ensure that cuttings are taken prior to the onset of frosty weather – perhaps in late September.

SEPTEMBER 1998

In spite of the lack of success in 1997, the experiment was set up again in September 1998. On this occasion the cuttings, each of about 1ft (30cm) in length, were removed from the plants in the last week of September. The foliage, which was still in excellent condition, was carefully removed making sure that there would be no damage to the dormant buds in the leaf axils.

Cuttings were treated with 'Roota', a hormonal rooting liquid, and placed in the corner of a cool greenhouse. The compost was watered when necessary (moist but not wet).

The results were again very satisfactory – all the cuttings rooted, although the majority produced shoots only from the tops. Nevertheless, they were produced in sufficient quantity and were of sufficient size to produce the early batch of cuttings.

CONCLUSIONS

This is an excellent and simple way of growing young mother plants to produce early cutting material. Also a very good way to send cutting material through the post – if you wrap the base of each stick in moist paper it will be quite safe for at least forty-eight hours. It has also been suggested that the method could be used to grow a 'mini-standard' quickly.

I hope to continue this experiment with one slight variation. I have noticed the method used for taking cuttings of roses, blackcurrants and other soft fruits and feel it might be advantageous to leave two or three sets of leaves at the top of each stick when planting them.

So far the cuttings have been overwintered in the corner of a frost-free greenhouse – planting in the open garden or in a covered cold frame might show interesting results although it is likely that the development of shoots would come later in the spring thus removing the undoubted advantage obtained from getting early cutting material.

CHAPTER 12

A–Z of Hardy Fuchsias

UNDERSTANDING THE DESCRIPTIONS

In the pages that follow, fuchsias that appear in the hardy collection of fuchsias at Silver Dale Nurseries, North Devon, are described.

The name of each cultivar is followed by the raiser and the date of raising. The description generally includes the colouring of the tube, the sepals and the petals in the corolla. The colouring of the foliage is also usually included. Strength of growth together with a rough estimate of the height that each plant is expected to reach is given. If the plant is accepted for show purposes as a 'showbench hardy' by the British Fuchsia Society, this will appear at the end of entry together with an indication of hardiness, based on observations made in North Devon. Please note that whilst these ratings will provide a useful guide, they may not always be true of an individual area.

❀ Hardy only in mild areas
❀❀ Hardy apart from the coldest areas
❀❀❀ Hardy in most areas
❀❀❀❀ Hardy throughout the country

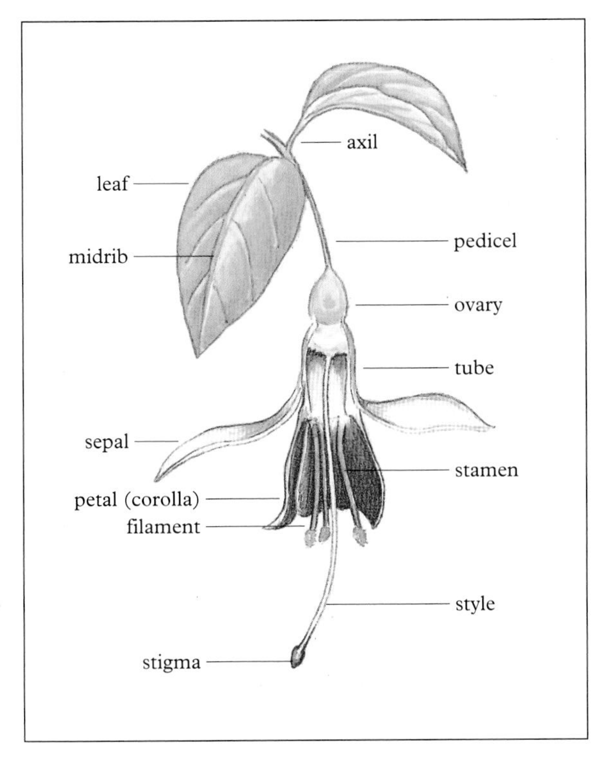

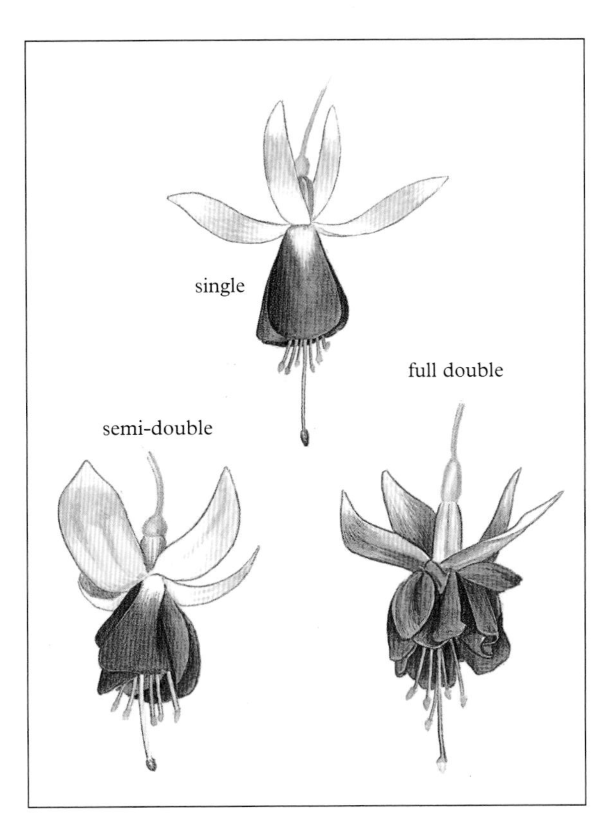

Reproductive organs of a fuchsia. (Right) *Types of flowers.*

A

Abbé Farges (Lemoine–France–1901) Light cerise sepals with rosy-lilac petals in the corolla. Small, semi-double flowers, profusely produced, and bushy growth. Mid-green foliage. Height 18in (45cm). BFS showbench hardy. ❀❀

Achievement (Melville–UK–1886) Reddish-cerise sepals, recurving back vertically. The petals in the corolla are reddish-purple. Medium to large, single flowers, very freely produced throughout the season. Yellowish-green foliage. Strong, upright and bushy growth. Height to 2ft (60cm). BFS showbench hardy. ❀❀

Admiration (Wood–UK–1940) Cardinal-red sepals. The petals in the corolla are ruby-red becoming lighter at the base. Medium, single flowers, freely produced. Moderate, olive-green foliage heavily veined deep red. Upright bush. Height 15–18in (37–45cm). BFS showbench hardy. ❀❀❀

Achievement.

Alfred Rambaud (Lemoine–France–1896) Scarlet sepals. The petals in the corolla are violet-purple maturing to rosy-purple. Very large, fully double flowers. Dark green foliage. Strong, upright and bushy growth. Height 18in (45cm). ❀❀

Alice Hoffman (Klese–Germany–1911) Rose sepals. The petals in the corolla are white, veined with rose. Small, semi-double flowers, very freely produced. Small, bronzy-green foliage. Upright, compact and bushy growth. Height 18in (45cm). BFS showbench hardy. ❀❀

Alison Sweetman (Roe–UK–1984) Strong, purplish-red sepals. The petals in the corolla are deep purple, veined and finely edged with purplish-red. Medium, single flowers, very freely produced. Mid-green foliage. Strong, upright, and bushy growth. Height 2ft (60cm). ❀❀

Amethyst Fire (Tabraham–UK–1975) Red sepals. The petals in the corolla are amethyst-blue, heavily splashed with pink. Large, double flowers, fairly freely produced. Strong, upright and bushy growth. Height 18in (45cm). ❀

A M Larwick (Smith–New Zealand–1940) The long, curling sepals are rich carmine. The petals in the corolla are purplish-mauve with a carmine vein. Medium, single flowers, freely produced. Mid-green foliage with red veining. Upright and bushy growth. Height 18in (45cm). BFS showbench hardy. ❀❀

Ariel (Encliandra Hybrid) (Travis–UK–1970) Magenta sepals with green tips. The petals in the corolla are deep magenta-pink. Very tiny, single flowers with tiny, glossy, dark green foliage. Growth is rather lax as a bush but will make an excellent miniature standard or, if used in topiary work, trained around wires. Height 2ft (60cm). ❀❀

Army Nurse (Hodges–USA–1947) Deep carmine sepals. The petals in the corolla are bluish-violet, veined with pink, and pink at the base. Fairly small,

Alice Hoffman.

(Below) *Amethyst Fire.*

(Above left) *A M Larwick.*
(Above) *Ariel (Encliandra Hybrid).*

Army Nurse.

Baby Blue Eyes.

(Below) *Baby Thumb.*

semi-double flowers carried in profusion. Upright and very bushy growth. Height 3–4ft (90–120cm). ❀❀❀

Avalanche (Henderson–UK–1869) Scarlet sepals. The petals in the corolla are purplish-violet splashed with carmine. Large, double flowers and yellowish-green foliage with red veining. Growth is rather lax so needs some support to form an upright bush. Height 2ft (60cm). ❀

B

Baby Blue Eyes (Plummer–USA–1952) Red sepals with dark lavender-blue petals in the corolla. Small, single flowers carried in profusion along the whole stem. Upright and bushy growth. Height 2ft (60cm) plus. BFS showbench hardy. ❀

Baby Thumb (Unknown) Light, reddish-carmine sepals. The petals in the corolla are white, veined with carmine. Very small, semi-double flowers, freely produced. Delightful cream and green foliage. Dwarf upright bush (variegated 'sport' of 'Lady Thumb'). Height 12in (30cm). ❀❀❀

Barbara (Tolley–UK–1971) Pale pink sepals. The petals in the corolla are cherry and tangerine-pink. Very attractive medium, single flowers with delicate colouring. Pale, rather dull green foliage. Strong, upright and vigorous growth. Will make a good standard but take in during the winter if used for border height. Height 3–4ft (90–120cm). ❀❀

Barry's Queen (Sheppard–UK–1980) Rhodamine-pink sepals with green tips. The petals in the corolla are violet flushed with pale pink, veined with dark pink. Medium, single flowers, freely produced with mid-green foliage. Upright, bushy growth. Height 18in (45cm). ❀

Bashful (Tabraham–UK–1974) Deep pink sepals. The petals in the corolla are white, veined with red. Small, double flowers, very freely produced. Strong, upright and bushy growth. Suitable for the front of a hardy border. Height 9–15in (22–38cm). BFS showbench hardy. ❀

Beacon (Bull–UK–1871) Deep pink sepals with bright mauvish-pink petals in the corolla. Medium, single flowers, very freely produced. Fairly dark green foliage with waved edging. Upright, bushy and compact growth. Height 2ft (60cm). BFS showbench hardy. ❀❀❀

Beacon Rosa (Burgi-Ott–Switzerland–1972) Deep pink sepals. The petals in the corolla are pink, lightly veined with red. Medium, single flowers. Fairly dark green foliage with waved edging. This 'sport' of 'Beacon' has a tendency to revert to its parental colouring and erring branches should be removed. Height 18in (45cm). ❀❀❀

Beauty of Clyffe Hall (Lye–UK–1881) Pale dawn-pink sepals. The petals in the corolla are strong purplish-red, paling towards the base. Medium to small, single flowers. The mid-green foliage is veined with red. Rather lax growth (best if supported with stakes). Height 18in (45cm). ❀❀

Beauty of Prussia (Holmes–UK–1966) Scarlet sepals. The petals in the corolla are scarlet lake, veined with deeper scarlet. Medium, double flowers, freely produced. Shiny, dark green foliage. Upright and bushy growth. Height 2ft (60cm). ❀❀

Bella Forbes (Forbes–UK–1890) Cerise sepals. The petals in the corolla are creamy-white, veined with cerise. Large, fully double flowers. The mid-green foliage is overlaid with bronze and has pale veins and stems. Height about 18in (45cm). ❀

Beranger (Lemoine–France–1897) Deep cerise sepals. The petals in the corolla are violet-blue splashed with cerise-purple. Small to medium, double flowers, freely produced. Mid-green foliage with slight brown vein. Small upright bush. Height 12in (30cm). ❀❀❀

Berliner Kind (Eggbrecht–Germany–1882) Scarlet-cerise sepals. The petals in the corolla are white, veined with pink. Small, double flowers, prolifically produced. Mid-green foliage. Upright and bushy growth. Height 15in (38cm). ❀❀

Beverley (Holmes–UK–1976) Neyron-rose sepals with green tips. The petals in the corolla are fuchsia-purple rose with a fine, deep burgundy edging. Medium, single flowers. Light green foliage. A vigorous, fast-growing bush. Height 2ft (60cm). ❀

Blue Beauty (Bull–UK–1854) Red sepals with bluish-violet petals in the corolla. Full, double blooms, freely produced. Mid-green foliage. Strong, upright bush that will make a good standard. Height 2½ft (75cm). ❀❀

Blue Bush (Gadsby–UK–1973) Rosy-red sepals. The petals in the corolla are bluebird blue fading to Bishop's violet with rose veins. Medium, single flowers, very freely produced. Fairly small, mid-green foliage. Strong, upright and bushy growth – will make a good hedge. Height 3–4ft (90–120cm). BFS showbench hardy. ❀❀❀

(Opposite Page)
(Top left) *Bashful.*
(Top right) *Beverley.*
(Bottom left) *Blue Beauty.*
(Bottom right) *Blue Bush.*

Blue Tit.

Blue Gown (Milne–UK) Cerise sepals. The petals in the corolla are bluish-purple, splashed with pink and carmine. Large, beautiful, double flowers, freely produced from early in the season. Mid-green foliage. Upright and vigorous growth. Will make an excellent standard. Height 2½ft (75cm). BFS showbench hardy. ❀❀❀

Blue Lace (Tabraham–UK–1974) Red sepals with blue petals in the corolla. Large, double flowers, continuously produced. Dark green foliage. Upright and bushy growth with a strong natural branching habit. Height 2ft (60cm). ❀

Blue Tit (Hobson–UK–1982) Red sepals. The petals in the corolla are violet, veined with red, with a pale pink splash at the base. Small, single flowers, produced in great profusion. Upright and vigorous growth. Height 15in (38cm). ❀

Bouquet (Lemoine–France–1893) Red sepals. The petals in the corolla are violet, maturing to a reddish-purple. Small, double flowers and foliage. The dwarf habit makes it a very good, prolific-flowering plant for the rockery. Height 12–15in (30–38cm). BFS showbench hardy. ❀❀

***F. brevilobis* (*Quelusia specie*)** (Brazil) (Berry–USA–1989) Long, red, tube-fused sepals almost enclosing the purple, tubular petals. Small, single flowers. Mid-green foliage with narrow leaves. Long-ranging branches stretch 3ft (90cm) or more. ❀❀

Brilliant (Bull–UK–1865) Scarlet sepals with violet-magenta petals in the corolla. Medium, single flowers, freely produced. Upright and bushy growth. Very vigorous – will make a good climber, but needs frequent pinching to produce a bush. Height 2½ft (75cm). BFS showbench hardy. ❀❀❀

Bouquet.

(Below) *Briony Caunt.*
(Below right) *Brodsworth.*

Briony Caunt (Caunt–UK–1987) Bright cardinal-red sepals. The petals in the corolla are vivid purple with a bright rose-red stripe or blotch. Medium, single flowers, freely produced. Moderate, green foliage with red veining. Upright and bushy growth. Height 2ft (60cm). ❀❀

Brodsworth (Nuttall–UK–1977) Cherry red to scarlet sepals. The petals in the corolla are very deep purple with a magenta vein. Medium, single flowers, freely produced. Dullish green foliage with a strong red vein. Self-branching, upright and bushy growth. Could be considered an improved

Caledonia.

(Below left) F. campos-portoi.
(Below) *Cardinal Farges.*

'Mrs Popple' from which it was a seedling × 'Neue Welt'. Height 2ft (60cm). ❀❀❀

Brutus (Bull–UK–1901) Rich cerise sepals. The petals in the corolla are rich dark purple. Medium, single flowers, very freely produced early in the season. Upright, bushy and vigorous growth. Height 2ft (60cm). BFS showbench hardy. ❀❀❀

C

Caledonia (Lemoine–France–1899) Cerise sepals with crimson petals in the corolla. Medium, single flowers, freely produced. Spreading and bushy growth. Height 2ft (60cm). BFS showbench hardy. ❀❀❀

***F. campos-portoi* (*Quelusia specie*)** (Pilzer & Schulze–Brazil–1935) Dark pink to red sepals with purple petals in the corolla. Small, single flowers with small, dark green, narrow and pointed foliage. Dwarf growth of height 12–15in (30–38cm), spread about 2ft (60cm). ❀

Carmen.

Cardinal Farges (Rawlins–UK–1958) Pale cerise sepals. The petals in the corolla are white, lightly veined with cerise. Small, semi-double flowers, very freely produced. Upright, bushy and vigorous growth. Tends to be rather brittle and branches break off easily. Height 15in (38cm). BFS showbench hardy. ❀

Carmen (Lemoine–France–1893) Glossy, cerise sepals. The petals in the corolla are purple with red veining, small petaloids are purple splashed with pink. Small, semi-double flowers, profusely produced. Mid-green foliage. Rather low growing, not exceeding about 15in (38cm). BFS showbench hardy. ❀❀❀

Carmine Bell (Caunt–UK–1985) Neyron-rose sepals, curling back on to a long thin tube. The petals in the corolla are rosy-carmine, edged with deeper rose. Medium, single, bell-shaped flowers. Large, mid-green foliage. Upright bush but tends to sprawl. Height 12–18in (30–45cm). ❀❀

Carmine Bell.

Carnea.

Charles Edward.

Carnea (Smith–UK–1861) Red sepals with purple petals in the corolla. Small, single flowers, freely produced. The sepals tend to open only about 25 per cent with the flared petals just showing. Small, pale yellowish-green foliage. Height 12in (30cm). BFS showbench hardy. ❀❀

Charming (Lye–UK–1877) Reddish-cerise sepals with rosy-purple petals in the corolla. Medium, single flowers, very freely produced. Yellowish foliage becoming very pale at the tips of the leaves. Upright and bushy growth. Height 2½ft (75cm). BFS showbench hardy. ❀❀❀

Charles Edward (Rolt–UK–1992) The sepals are carmine through white, veined with carmine, recurved and upward twisting. The petals in the corolla are violet with a white base and carmine veining. Medium, double flowers. Lightish green foliage. Upright, bushy growth. Height 2ft (60cm). ❀❀

Chillerton Beauty (Bass–UK–1847) Pale, rose-pink sepals. The petals in the corolla are mauvish-violet, veined with pink. Small, single flowers, very freely produced. Upright and bushy growth. Height 3ft (90cm). BFS showbench hardy. ❀❀❀

China Lantern (USA–*c.*1953) White sepals with green tips. The petals in the corolla are rosy-pink with white at the base. Medium, single flowers, freely produced. Dark green foliage. Upright but lax, bushy growth. Height 2ft (60cm). BFS showbench hardy. ❀❀

C J Howlett (Howlett–UK–1911) Reddish-pink sepals. The petals in the corolla are bluish-carmine, heavily veined with carmine from the base. Small, single flowers produced early and freely. Upright and bushy growth. Height to about 15in (38cm). BFS showbench hardy. ❀❀

Cliff's Hardy (Gadsby–UK–1966) The sepals are carmine paling to green towards the tip. The petals in the corolla open strongly purple, paling towards the base. Medium, single flowers, freely produced. Mid- to dark green foliage. Upright and bushy growth. Height 18–24in (45–60cm). BFS showbench hardy. ❀❀❀

(Right) *China Lantern.*

(Below) *Cliff's Hardy.*

(Above) *Clifton Charm.*

Clifton Charm (Hadley–UK–1981) The sepals are bright cerise fading to light cerise. The petals in the corolla are deep lilac-rose with a pinkish base and red veining and edging. Medium, single, bell-shaped flowers. Mid- to dark green foliage with a paler vein. Upright, bushy growth. Height 18in (45cm). ❀❀

Clipper (Lye–UK–1897) Cerise sepals. The petals in the corolla are purple with a cerise base and vein, maturing to claret. Medium, single flowers, freely produced. Mid-green foliage with red stems. Upright and bushy growth. Height 18in (45cm). ❀❀

***F. coccinea* (*Quelusia specie*)** (Brazil–1789) Scarlet-red sepals with violet-purple petals in the corolla. Small, single flowers with dull, light green foliage. Rather willowy and spreading. Height 2½ft (75cm). ❀❀

Connie (Dawson–UK–1961) Cerise-red sepals. The petals in the corolla are white, veined and flushed cerise. Medium to large, double flowers, with light green foliage. Upright and bushy growth. Height 2½ft (75cm). BFS showbench hardy. ❀

Conspicua (Smith–UK–1863) Bright scarlet sepals. The petals in the corolla are white, veined with

Connie.

(Above left) *Conspicua.*
(Above) *Constance.*
(Left) *Copycat.*

scarlet. Small, single or sometimes semi-double flowers, very profuse. Upright and bushy growth. Height 2ft (60cm). BFS showbench hardy. ❀❀

Constance (Berkeley Hort Nursery–USA–1935) Soft pink sepals. The petals in the corolla are bluish-mauve with a pink tinge. Medium, double flowers, freely produced. Upright and bushy growth. Height 18in (45cm). BFS showbench hardy. ❀

Copycat (Stubbs–USA–1981) Rose-red sepals. The petals in the corolla are lavender-blue with very pale pink bases and rose veins. Small, single flowers,

(Above left) *Corallina.*
(Above) *Cottinghamii.*
(Left) *Cupid.*

freely produced with mid-green foliage. Upright, bushy growth. Height to about 2ft (60cm). ❀

Corallina (Pince–UK–1884) Scarlet sepals. The petals in the corolla are rich purple with a pink base. Medium, single or double flowers. Dark green, bronze-tinted foliage. Very vigorous, lax, spreading bush. Height 3ft (90cm) and spread of 3–4ft (90–120cm). BFS showbench hardy. ❀❀❀❀

Cottinghamii (Unknown) Pink sepals with green tips. Very small, single, encliandra-type flowers are perpetually in bloom. Small, mid-green foliage. Strong, upright growth. Height 2ft (60cm). ❀

Cupid (Brown–UK–1929) Light scarlet-cerise sepals. The petals in the corolla are bluish-magenta, paling towards the base, with cerise veining. Small, single flowers, prolifically produced. Mid-green foliage on a dwarf, upright growing plant. Height 12in (30cm). ❀

D

David (Wood–UK–1937) Cerise-red sepals. The petals in the corolla are rich purple with red bases and veins. Small, single flowers and foliage that is mid-green on the upper surface and pale green below. Dwarf bush. Height 12in (30cm). ❀❀

Delta's Wonder (Vreeke–The Netherlands–1989) Reddish-purple sepals. The petals in the corolla are lilac with red and purple stripes. Large, single flowers, continuously produced. Growth is rather lax for a bush and will require staking. Height 18in (45cm). ❀❀

Diana Wright (Wright–UK–1984) Pink sepals with green tips. The petals in the corolla are phlox-pink. Small, single flowers, very freely produced. Dark green foliage. Upright and bushy growth. Height 2ft (60cm). ❀❀❀

David.

Delta's Wonder.

Dimples.

(Below) *Doc.*

Dimples (Storvick–USA–1981) Red sepals. The petals in the corolla are white, splashed and veined with magenta. Small, double flowers, freely produced. Mid-green foliage. Lax, bushy growth. Height 12in (30cm). ❀

Display (Smith–UK–1881) Rose-pink sepals. The petals in the corolla are a deeper shade of pink. Medium, single flowers. An early blooming plant which continues throughout the season. Excels as a bush but can also be used for larger structures. Height 18in (45cm) (when grown as a bush). BFS showbench hardy. ❀❀

Doc (Tabraham–UK–1974) Red sepals with pale purple petals in the corolla. Small, single flowers, extremely free and continuous. Deep green foliage. Upright and bushy growth. Dwarf bush with height of 9–15in (23–38cm). BFS showbench hardy. ❀

Dollar Princess (Lemoine–France–1912) Cerise sepals. The petals in the corolla, which remain tightly folded, are rich purple. Small to medium, fully double flowers, very profuse. Darkish green foliage. Upright, strong and vigorous growth. Useful for all types of upward training. Height 18in (45cm). BFS showbench hardy. ❀❀❀

Dopy (Tabraham–UK–1974) Red sepals. The petals in the corolla are purple, tinged with pink. Small, double flowers very freely produced. Dark green foliage. Upright and bushy growth on dwarf plants. Height 9–15in (23–38cm). BFS showbench hardy. ❀

Dorothy (Wood–UK–1946) Bright crimson sepals. The petals in the corolla are violet with pale bases and red veins. Medium, single flowers, freely produced. Darkish green foliage with red veins and stems. Can reach a height of 3ft (90cm). BFS showbench hardy. ❀

Dorothea Flower (Thornley–UK–1969) The sepals are white with a faint flesh-pink flush, darker underneath. The petals in the corolla are violet-blue, flushed pink at the base. Small, single flowers produced in great profusion. Upright and bushy growth. Best in a sun-sheltered spot. Height 18in (45cm). ❀

Drame (Lemoine–France–1880) Scarlet sepals with violet-purple petals in the corolla. Medium, semi-double flowers, freely produced. Yellowish-green foliage. Upright, bushy and spreading growth. Will make a good hedge. Height 2ft (60cm). BFS showbench hardy. ❀❀❀❀

Dr Foster (Lemoine–France–1899) Scarlet sepals with violet petals in the corolla. Large flowers, freely

Dorothy.

Dorothea Flower.

Dr Foster.

Duchess of Cornwall.

Edith.

produced. Mid-green foliage. Upright and bushy growth. Height 3ft (90cm). BFS showbench hardy. ❀❀

Duchess of Cornwall (Tabraham–UK–1986) Bright red sepals with pure white petals in the corolla. Very large, double flowers. Dark green foliage. Slightly lax and soft growth so could be used in hanging containers. Will need staking in an open border. Height 18in (45cm). ❀

E

Edith (Brown–UK–1980) Red sepals with lavender petals in the corolla. Medium, semi-double flowers. Upright and vigorous growth. A 'sport' from 'Margaret' and delightful in every way. Height 3–4ft (90–120cm). ❀❀❀

Eileen Saunders (Holmes–UK–1974) Crimson sepals, tipped with green. The petals in the corolla are fuchsia-purple with a carmine base and veining. Bell-shaped, single flowers with reflexing sepals. Mid-green foliage. Upright and bushy growth. Height 15in (38cm). ❀

El Cid (Colville–UK–1966) Deep red sepals with burgundy-red petals in the corolla. Medium, single flowers, profuse and well shaped. Upright and bushy growth. Height 18in (45cm). BFS showbench hardy. ❀❀

El Cid.

(Below) *Eleanor Rawlins.*

Eleanor Rawlins (Wood–UK–1954) Carmine sepals. The petals in the corolla open violet with a pale pink base and carmine veins, and mature to magenta. Medium, single flowers with long slender sepals. Mid- to light green foliage. Upright bush. Height 15in (38cm). BFS showbench hardy. ❀❀

Elfin Glade (Colville–UK–1963) The sepals are pink with a rosy tint. The petals in the corolla are pinkish-mauve, veined pink. Medium, single flowers, freely produced. Upright and bushy growth. Height 15in (38cm). ❀❀

Elfrida (Miellez–France–1871) Red sepals with green tips. The petals in the corolla are purple with a rose-pink splash. Medium, double flowers. Mid-green foliage on a strong, upright bush. Height 18in (45cm). ❀❀

Empress of Prussia (Hoppe–UK–1868) Glowing scarlet sepals. The petals in the corolla are reddish-magenta with slight paling at the base. Large, single flowers. Very floriferous – each joint carries six to

(Above) *Elfin Glade.*

Elfrida.

eight blooms. Strong, upright and bushy growth. Height up to 3ft (90cm). BFS showbench hardy. ❀❀❀

Enfant Prodigue (Lemoine–France–1887) Crimson sepals. The petals in the corolla are bluish-purple, maturing to magenta. Medium, semi-double flowers, very freely produced. Upright and bushy growth. Height 2ft (60cm). BFS showbench hardy. ❀❀❀

Eric's Hardy (Weeks–UK–1986) White sepals with a pink base. The petals in the corolla open dark blue with a white to pink base, maturing to mauve-pink with a white base. Mid-green foliage. Inclined to be lax so needs support. Height 15in (38cm). ❀❀

Ernest Rankin (Wright–UK–1987) Aubergine-pink sepals with aubergine-purple petals in the corolla. Medium to small, single flowers. Mid-green foliage on strong and upright bushes. Height 18in (45cm). ❀❀

Eva Boerg (Yorke–UK–1943) Pinkish-white sepals. The petals in the corolla are pinkish-purple, splashed with pink. Medium, single to semi-double flowers, freely produced. Lightish-green foliage. Lax, low bush – could be used in hanging containers. Height to 18in (45cm). ❀

F. excorticata (Skinnera specie) (Forster–New Zealand–1776) The sepals are green turning to purple. The petals in the corolla are purplish-black. Bright blue pollen. Large, dark green, glossy leaves. Strong, upright growth. Height 3ft (90cm). ❀

F

Falklands (Dunnett–UK–1984) White sepals shading to roseine. The petals in the corolla are fuchsia-purple maturing to rose-bengal. Half flared, medium, semi-double flowers. Mid-green foliage. Upright bush. Height to 2ft (60cm). BFS showbench hardy. ❀❀

(Above) *Empress of Prussia.*

Falklands.

Flash.

Flying Cloud.

Flash (Hazard & Hazard–USA–1930) Light magenta sepals. The petals in the corolla are light magenta-red. Small, single flowers, very profuse. Small, light green foliage. Upright, vigorous and bushy growth. Height 2½ft (75cm). BFS showbench hardy. ❀❀

Florence Turner (Turner–UK–1955) White sepals. The petals in the corolla are pale pinkish-purple. Medium, single flowers, produced early and freely. Upright and bushy growth. Height 2½ft (75cm). BFS showbench hardy. ❀❀

Flying Cloud (Reiter–USA–1949) The sepals are white, tipped with green, with a faint pink sheen on the underside. The petals in the corolla are white, touched with pink at the base. Large, double flowers, freely produced. Lax, upright growth on spreading bushes. Height 18in (45cm). BFS showbench hardy. ❀

Foxgrove Wood (Stiff–UK–1990) The sepals are pale green, with cerise streaks and green tips. The petals in the corolla are lilac-blue, veined with cerise. Small but prolific single flowers. Dull, mid-green foliage, lax on an upright bush. Height 15in (38cm). ❀

Frau Hilde Rademacher (Rademacher–Germany–1925) Rich red sepals. The petals in the corolla are lilac blue/cerise. Medium, double flowers, freely produced. Lax, spreading bush. Height 18in (45cm). ❀

Foxgrove Wood.

(Below) *Frau Hilde Rademacher.*

Fred's First.

Fred's First (Wooley–UK–1978) The sepals and tube are a deep purplish-pink. The sepals curve back to touch the tube. The petals in the corolla are vivid purple, veined with rose-bengal. Medium, double flowers. Mid-green foliage on a self-branching, upright bush. Height 18in (45cm). ❀❀❀

Fruhling (Elsner–Austria–1878) Light red sepals that remain down – only half opening. The petals in the corolla are purple streaked with red. Medium to large double blooms, free-flowering. Mid-green foliage on an upright bush. Height 12–15in (30–38cm). ❀

Fuksie Foetsie (Van der Grijp–The Netherlands–1979) The sepals are white, shading to flesh-pink, maturing to pinky-violet. The petals in the corolla are white, maturing to pale pink. Very small, single, encliandra-type flowers. Small, mid- to dark green foliage on a spreading bush. Height 2ft (60cm). ❀❀

Fuksie Foetsie.

G

Garden News (Handley–UK–1978) Pink sepals. The petals in the corolla are magenta-rose with rose-pink at the base. Large, double flowers, continuously produced from early in the season. Mid-green, slightly serrated foliage. Upright and bushy growth. Height 2ft (60cm). BFS showbench hardy. ❀❀❀

General Monk (Unknown–France–1844) Cerise-rose sepals. The petals in the corolla are blue, maturing to mauvish-blue. Medium, double flowers, very free and open. Height 18in (45cm). BFS showbench hardy. ❀❀

General Voyron (Lemoine–France–1901) Cerise sepals. The petals in the corolla are violet overlaid with magenta, with a pink base and cerise veins.

Small petaloids splashed pink. Medium, single flowers. Mid-green foliage with red veins. Upright and bushy growth. Height 2ft (60cm). ❀❀

Genii (Jeane) (Reiter–USA–1951) Cerise sepals. The petals in the corolla are rich violet with a pink base and cerise veins. Small, single flowers, very freely produced. The most attractive feature is the yellow foliage with red stems. Strong, upright and bushy – will make a good hedge. Height 2ft (60cm). BFS showbench hardy. ❀❀❀

Geoffrey Smith (Bielby–UK–1987) The sepals are crimson on the underside and neyron-rose beneath. The petals in the corolla are neyron-rose with strong crimson veining. Small, rounded, double flowers, very prolific. Upright growth although dwarf. Height to about 12in (30cm). ❀❀

Gerald Drewitt (Weeks–UK–1984) The sepals are pale pink with a dark pink blush. The petals in the corolla are grey-blue with a rose base. Small, single blooms flower early in the season. Mid-green

(Above) *General Monk.*
(Above right) *Geoffrey Smith.*
(Right) *Gerald Drewitt.*

F. glazioviana.

(Below) *Glow.*

foliage. Upright, bushy growth. Worth trying as a standard. Height 18in (45cm). ❀

F. glazioviana (Quelusia specie) (Taubert–Brazil–1888) Rhodamine sepals with a purplish hue. The petals in the corolla are reddish-purple. Very small single flowers. Mid-green, glossy foliage on a spreading bush. Height 20in (50cm). ❀❀❀

Glow (Wood–UK–1946) Red sepals. The petals in the corolla are burgundy/purple overlaid with scarlet, with a scarlet base. Medium, single flowers. Dull, mid-green foliage with red veining. Long, willowy stems. Height 2ft (60cm). BFS showbench hardy. ❀❀❀

Gold Brocade (Tabraham–UK–1976) Red sepals with mauve petals in the corolla. Large, single flowers, very freely produced. Deep, golden-green foliage, heavily veined with purple. Upright, strong and bushy growth. Height 2ft (60cm). BFS showbench hardy. ❀

Golden Lena (Pacey–UK–1979) Pale flesh-pink sepals. The petals in the corolla are rosy-magenta pink. Medium, semi-double flowers, freely produced. Varying shades of green and gold foliage. Lax bush, will trail. Height 15in (38cm). ❀

Gold Brocade.

(Below) *Golden Melody.*
(Below right) *Golondrina.*

Golden Melody (Tabraham–UK–1976) Deep pink sepals with blue-lavender petals in the corolla. Medium, fully double flowers. Deep green/gold foliage. Upright, strong and bushy growth. Height 18in (45cm). ❀

Golden Treasure (Carter–UK–1860) Scarlet sepals. The petals in the corolla are purple with a slightly pink base and cerise veining. Small, single flowers. Pale golden-green foliage, some variegated yellow and pale green with a red vein. Small bush. Height 15in (38cm). ❀❀❀

Goldsworth Beauty (Slocock–UK–1952) Pale cerise sepals with reddish-purple petals in the corolla. Medium, single flowers, freely produced. Upright and bushy growth. Height 18in (45cm). BFS showbench hardy. ❀❀

Golondrina (Niederholzer–USA–1941) Rose-madder sepals. The petals in the corolla are magenta streaked with light pink and crimson blotches. Medium, single flowers. Mid-green foliage on a rather lax, low-growing bush. Height 15in (38cm). ❀

Grey Lady.

Graf Witte (Lemoine–France–1899) Carmine sepals with purple petals in the corolla. Small, single but profusely flowering blooms. Yellowish-green foliage with crimson midrib and veins. Medium bush. Height 3ft (90cm). BFS showbench hardy. ❀❀❀

Grayrigg (Thornley–UK–1971) Blush pink sepals, tipped with green. The petals in the corolla are palest blue, lightly veined with pink, and a pink base. Medium, single flowers. Light green foliage with a paler vein. Upright bush. Height 2ft (60cm). BFS showbench hardy. ❀❀❀

Grey Lady (Tabraham–UK–1974) The sepals are red – clear magenta. The petals in the corolla are blue-grey, veined with magenta. Small, beautifully coloured double flowers. Mid- to dark green foliage with a red vein. Stiff upright growth. Height 2ft (60cm). ❀

Grumpy (Tabraham–UK–1974) Deep pink sepals with navy blue petals in the corolla. Small, single flowers are profuse. The most difficult of the dwarfs to overwinter as it does not like to be too wet. Height 9–15in (23–38cm). BFS showbench hardy. ❀

Gustave Dore (Lemoine–France–1880) Pink-cerise sepals. The petals in the corolla are white, veined with cerise. Medium, double flowers with pointed petals. Mid- to dark green foliage with red veins and stems. Height 18in (45cm). ❀❀

H

Hanser's Flight (Goulding–UK–1990) White sepals with a pink flush, and green tips. The petals in the corolla are pale lavender with a white base. Medium, single flowers. Mid- to dark green foliage with paler veins and red stems. Long-jointed and upright in growth. Height 2ft (60cm) plus. ❀

Happy (Tabraham–UK–1974) Red sepals with blue petals in the corolla. Small, single flowers, very freely produced. Pale green foliage. Upright and bushy dwarf. Height 9–15in (23–38cm). BFS showbench hardy. ❀

Happy Fellow (Walx–USA–1966) Light orange and pale salmon sepals. The petals in the corolla are orange and smokey-rose. Medium, single flowers, extremely freely produced. Light green foliage. Upright and bushy growth. Height 18in (45cm). ❀❀❀

F. hartwegii* *(Fuchsia specie) (Bentham–Colombia–1845) The sepals and the petals in the corolla are both orange. Small to medium, single, funnel-shaped flowers. Dark green foliage. Makes good growth but can be a little shy to produce its flowers. Height 2ft (60cm). ❀❀

F. hatschbachii* *(Quelusia specie) (Berry–Brazil–1989) Red sepals with violet petals in the corolla. Small, single flowers carried singly in leaf axils. Dark green foliage. Forms wiry stems extending to about 2½ft (75cm) in a season. ❀❀

Hawkshead (Travis–UK–1962) The sepals and the petals in the corolla are both a clean white. Small, single flowers. Small, dark green foliage with serrated leaves. Upright and bushy growth. Height 4ft (1.2m). ❀❀❀

Happy Fellow.

(Below) *Hawkshead.*

(Top) *Hemsleyana.*
(Bottom) *Heritage.*

Heidi Ann (Smith–UK–1969) Crimson sepals. The petals in the corolla are bright lilac, veined with cerise. Medium, double flowers, very freely produced. Dark green foliage with a crimson mid-rib. Upright and bushy growth. Height 18in (45cm). ❀❀❀

Hemsleyana (Woodson and Siebert–Costa Rica and Panama–1937) An encliandra-type fuchsia with minute purplish-rose flowers borne solitary in leaf axils. Upright shrub growing to several feed in natural habitat. Height 3ft (90cm). ❀❀

Herald (Sankey–UK–1887) Scarlet sepals. The petals in the corolla are deep purple. Medium, single flowers, very freely produced. Upright and bushy growth. Height 2ft (60cm). BFS showbench hardy. ❀❀❀

Heritage (Lemoine–France–1902) Scarlet sepals. The petals in the corolla are rich purple maturing to reddish-purple. Medium to large, semi-double flowers, freely produced. A rather slow grower. Height 15–18in (38–45cm). ❀❀

Heron (Lemoine–France–1891) Deep scarlet sepals. The petals in the corolla are violet-blue, veined and streaked with red. Large, single flowers, very freely produced. Upright, strong and bushy growth. Height 18in (45cm). ❀❀

H G Brown (Wood–UK–1946) Deep scarlet sepals with dark lake petals in the corolla. Small to medium, single flowers, profusely produced. Glossy, dark green foliage. Low and bushy growth. Height 12–15in (30–38cm). BFS showbench hardy. ❀❀❀

Howlett's Hardy (Howlett–UK–1952) Scarlet sepals. The petals in the corolla are violet-purple, veined with scarlet. Large, single flowers, fairly freely produced. Growth is as a medium bush. Height 3ft (90cm). BFS showbench hardy. ❀❀

I

Isis (Lemoine–France–1880) The sepals and the petals in the corolla are both crimson. An encliandra-type fuchsia with very small, single flowers. Small, dark green foliage. Upright growing, makes a very attractive bush. Height 18in (45cm). ❀❀

J

James Travis (Thorne–UK–1960) Bright cardinal-red sepals. The petals in the corolla are vivid purple shading to crimson, with a slight vein. Medium, double flowers, profusely produced. Moderate green foliage. Upright, bushy growth. Height 18in (45cm). ❀❀

(Above) *Isis.*

James Travis.

(Above left) *Jean Baker.*
(Above) *Jester.*

John E Caunt.

Janet Williams (Tabraham–UK–1976) Strong purplish-red sepals. The petals in the corolla are vivid violet, veined with rose-red. Medium, semi-double flowers. Lettuce-green foliage veined with dark red and overlaid with bronze. Growth is as an upright bush. Height 15in (38cm). ❀

Jean Baker (Weeks–UK–1984) Carmine sepals with pale green tips. The petals in the corolla are dark lilac/violet with a bluish-pink base and carmine veins. Small, single flowers with sepals curling back. Mid-green foliage. Height 15in (38cm). ❀

Jester (Holmes–UK–1968) Cerise sepals. The petals in the corolla are rich royal-purple. Medium, semi-double flowers. Mid-green foliage. Upright, bushy and fast-growing. Height 2ft (60cm). ❀❀

Joan Cooper (Wood–UK–1964) Pale rose-opal sepals with cherry red petals in the corolla. Small but plentiful single flowers. Light green foliage. Upright and bushy growth. Height 18in (45cm). BFS showbench hardy. ❀❀

John E Caunt (Caunt–UK–1994) Rose-red sepals, tipped with green. The petals in the corolla are deep purplish-pink, edged with fuchsia-purple and veined with red. Medium, single flowers. Dark green foliage. Upright, bushy growth. Height 18in (45cm). ❀❀

Justin's Pride (Jones–UK–1974) Neyron-rose sepals with deep cerise-pink petals in the corolla. Medium, single flowers, freely produced. Upright and bushy growth. Height 18in (45cm). BFS showbench hardy. ❀❀

K

Karen Siegers (Stoel–The Netherlands–1991) Pale red sepals. The petals in the corolla are reddish-mauve with a red base. Dark green foliage, single flowers with rather ragged, pointed petals, and a wide, very heavy, red tube make this a rather unusual flower. Fairly lax growth. Height 15in (38cm). ❀

Kenny Dalglish (Jones–UK–1988) Scarlet sepals. The petals in the corolla are purple, veined with red. Medium, double flowers are produced very freely throughout the season. Strong, upright growth. Height 3ft (90cm). ❀❀❀

L

Lady Boothby (Rafill–UK–1939) Crimson sepals with blackish-purple petals in the corolla. Small, single flowers, very freely produced in the leaf axils. Dark green foliage. Its natural desire is to climb and clamber through upright structures when 'unstopped'. Very vigorous – will cover an archway in a season. As a 'trained' bush will grow to about 2ft (60cm). BFS showbench hardy. ❀❀

Lady Boothby.

Lady Thumb (Roe–UK–1966) Light reddish-carmine sepals. The petals in the corolla are white, veined with crimson. Very small, semi-double flowers, freely produced. Small foliage. Growth is as an upright dwarf plant (a sport from 'Tom Thumb'). Height 12–18in (30–45cm). BFS showbench hardy. ❀❀❀❀

Lechlade Magician (Wright–UK–1986) Purplish-carmine sepals with dark purple petals in the corolla. Medium, single flowers, very freely produced. Dark green foliage. Growth, once established, is best described as rampant – a bush can be trained to 3ft (90cm) in a season. ❀❀

Lena (Bunney–UK–1862) Flesh-pink sepals with rose-magenta petals in the corolla. Medium, semi-double flowers, very freely produced. Mid-green foliage. Growth is rather lax for a bush – suitable for hanging containers. Height 18in (45cm). BFS showbench hardy. ❀❀

Liebriez (Kohene–Germany–1974) Pale cerise sepals. The petals in the corolla are pinkish-white, veined with pink. Small, semi-double flowers, profusely produced. Upright and bushy growth. Height 12in (30cm). BFS showbench hardy. ❀❀❀

Liz (Holmes–UK–1970) Pale pink sepals with green tips. The petals in the corolla are pale pink with deep pink veining. Medium, double flowers and mid-green foliage. Strong, upright and bushy growth. Height 18in (45cm). ❀❀

Logan Woods (Discovered in Logan Gardens, Scotland) Red tube. The green-tipped sepals are white blushed with pink. The petals in the corolla are violet with a pink base and veins. Prolific, small, single flowers. Small, mid-green foliage. Height 2–3ft (60–90cm). ❀❀❀❀

Lottie Hobby (Hybrid × *F. bacillaris*) (Edwards–UK–1839) Crimson sepals with dark crimson petals in the corolla. The tiny, single flowers are held erect. Glossy, dark green, tiny foliage. Very upright and vigorous growth. Ideal to train around wires for topiary work. When trained as a bush will achieve 18–24in(45–60cm). ❀

F. lycioides* × *F. magellanica Light crimson sepals with light purple petals in the corolla. Small, single flowers are produced in profusion at the end of each branch. Mid-green foliage with elliptic-ovate leaves. Height 3ft (90cm). ❀❀❀

Logan Woods.

F. lycioides × F. magellanica.

Lynne Marshall.

Lynne Marshall (Tabraham–UK–1974) Light purplish-pink sepals, tipped with green. The petals in the corolla are strong violet, paling towards the base. Medium, single flowers. The young foliage is yellowish-green maturing to olive-green. Strong upright bush. Height 2–2½ft (60–75cm). ❀

M

Macrostema (*magellanica* variety) Single flowers with scarlet tube and sepals. Corolla dark purple. Slightly larger flowers than most other *magellanica* varieties. Olive green foliage. Strong upright growth. Height to about 3ft (90cm). ❀❀❀❀

Madame Cornelissen (Cornelissen–Belgium–1860) Rich scarlet sepals. The petals in the corolla are white, veined with cerise. Smallish, semi-double flowers, very freely produced. Dark green foliage. Strong, upright and bushy growth. Excellent for

Macrostema.

F. magellanica.

hedging. Height 3ft (90cm). BFS showbench hardy. ❀❀❀

F. magellanica (Quelusia specie) (Lamarck–Chile–1788) Red sepals with purple-blue petals in the corolla. Small, single flowers, very freely produced. Foliage quite small. Vigorous, bushy growth. Excellent for hedging. Height 4ft (1.2m) plus. BFS showbench hardy. ❀❀❀❀

F. *magellanica* varieties
(all are BFS showbench hardy)

var. *Alba variegata* White sepals with pale pink petals in the corolla. Small, single flowers, very freely produced. Variegated gold and green foliage. Not quite as hardy as other *magellanica* variants. Height 2½ft (75cm). ❀❀❀

var. *Aurea* Scarlet sepals with purple petals in the corolla. Single flowers with bright golden-yellow foliage. Height 2½ft (75cm). ❀❀❀❀

var. *Conica* Carmine sepals with a turkey-red reverse. The tubular-shaped petals in the corolla are dark purple. Moderate olive-green foliage on an upright bush. Height 4ft (1.2m). ❀❀❀❀

var. *Globosa* Scarlet sepals with purple petals in the corolla. Small, single flowers, very freely produced. Dark green foliage with red stems. Strong grower. Height 3ft (90cm). ❀❀❀❀

var. *Gracilis* Scarlet-red sepals with purple petals in the corolla. Smallish, single flowers. Mid-green foliage. Upright and vigorous growth. Long, spreading branches. Height/spread about 6ft (1.8m). ❀❀❀❀

(Above left) *var.* Molinae (alba).
(Above) *var.* Alba variegata.
(Left) *var.* Globosa.

var. *Gracilis Tricolor* (Potney–UK–1840) Red sepals with purple petals in the corolla. Small, single flowers, very freely produced. Foliage is variegated cream, green and pink with red veining. Suitable as a hedge. Height 3ft (90cm). ❀❀❀❀

var. *Longipedunculata* Single flowers with red tube and sepals. The petals in the corolla are

var. Gracilis Tricolor.

(Below) *var.* Longipedunculata.

mauve. Small flowers carried on very long stalks or pedicels. Mid- to dark green foliage on bushy growth. Height to about 3ft (90cm). ❀❀❀❀

var. *Molinae (alba)* White sepals. The petals in the corolla are white, flushed pink. Very small, single flowers, but very free. Foliage is also small. In southern areas, or areas favoured with the warmth from the Gulf Stream, will grow to a height of 12–15ft (3.6–4.5m) with a spread of approximately 8ft (2.4m) in just four years. Makes a good hedge. A height of 4ft (1.2m) can be achieved in the first year. ❀❀❀❀

var. *Prostrata* (Scholfield–UK–1841) Dull red sepals. The bell-shaped petals in the corolla are violet with a red base, maturing to a reddish-purple. Single flowers and mid-green foliage with pale veins and reverse. Growth is as a low, spreading bush. Height 18in (45cm). ❀❀❀❀

var. *Pumilla* Scarlet sepals with mauve petals in the corolla. Very small, single flowers. Tiny plant ideally suitable for rockeries. Height 12in (30cm). ❀❀❀❀

(Above) *var.* Prostrata.
(Above right) *var.* Pumilla.

var. Ricartonii.

var. *Ricartonii* (Young–UK–1830) Scarlet sepals with dark purple petals in the corolla. Produces a display of single flowers that completely covers the whole bush. It will make a superb hedge. Height 4ft (1.2m). In favoured areas can reach a height of 15ft (4½m) with a width of 12ft (3.6m). ❀❀❀❀

var. *Rosea* Scarlet sepals with rose-pink petals in the corolla. Very small, single flowers, profusely produced. Small, mid-green foliage. Upright growth to about 2½ft (75cm). ❀❀❀❀

var. *Sharpitor* (National Trust–UK–1974) Palest mauve sepals with pink petals in the corolla. Very

var. Rosea.

(Below left) *var.* Thompsonii.
(Below) *var.* Variegata.

small, single flowers, very freely produced. Small, variegated cream and pale green foliage. A foliage 'sport' from *megallanica Alba.* Height 3ft (90cm). ❀❀❀❀

var. *Thompsonii* Scarlet sepals with pale purple petals in the corolla. Small, single flowers. Medium, grey-green foliage. Height 2ft (60cm). ❀❀❀❀

var. *Variegata* Crimson sepals with purple petals in the corolla. Small, single flowers. Pale green, cream-edged foliage, with a red hue to the young growing tips. Reddish-brown stems. Low-growing bush to about 18in (45cm) in height. ❀❀❀❀

var. *Versicolor* Tube and sepals red with purple petals in the corolla. Small flowers. Mainly grown for its attractive coloured foliage of dusty green-pink and red. Upright growing bush. Height about 3ft (90cm). ❀❀❀❀

Margaret (Wood–UK–1937) Carmine-scarlet sepals. The petals in the corolla are violet, veined

var. Versicolor.

Margaret.

Margaret Brown.

(Below) *Margaret Roe.*

with cerise. Medium, semi-double flowers, very freely produced. Upright, bushy and vigorous growth. Suitable for hedges. Height 4ft (1.2m). In mild winters with very little die-back will grow on to make a superb bush up to 8ft (2.4m) high. BFS showbench hardy. ❀❀❀

Margaret Brown (Wood–UK–1949) Rosy-pink sepals with light rose-bengal petals in the corolla. Smallish, single flowers, very freely produced. Light green foliage. Upright, bushy and vigorous growth. Will make a good low hedge. Height 2–3ft (60–90cm). BFS showbench hardy. ❀❀❀

Margaret Roe (Gadsby–UK–1968) Rosy-red sepals with pale violet-purple petals in the corolla. Free-flowering, medium, single blooms held horizontally to upright. Good bushy growth. Height 18in (45cm). BFS showbench hardy. ❀❀

Margarite Dawson.

(Below) *Mary Thorne.*

Margarite Dawson (Dawson–UK–1984) White sepals blushed with pink. The petals in the corolla are white with slight dark pink veining. Large, round, fully double flowers. Mid-green foliage with red veining. Height 15in (38cm). ❀❀

Margery Blake (Wood–UK–1950) Scarlet sepals with reddish-purple petals in the corolla. Small, compact, single flowers, prolifically and continuously produced. Upright and bushy growth. Height 15in (38cm). BFS showbench hardy. ❀❀

Mary Thorne (Thorne–UK–1954) Turkey-red sepals. The petals in the corolla are violet, maturing to reddish-purple with scarlet veining. Medium, single blooms, very free-flowering. Roundish, dark green foliage with a paler vein. Short-jointed and upright bushy growth. Height 18in (45cm). ❀❀❀

Mauve Beauty (Banks–UK–1869) Cerise sepals. The petals in the corolla open violet-purple with red veining and fade with maturity. Medium, double flowers, freely produced. Dark green foliage

(Above) *Mauve Beauty.*

Meditation.

with heavy red veining and stems. Height just under 3ft (90cm). ❀❀

Mauve Lace ((Tabraham–UK–1974) Red sepals with mauve petals in the corolla. Large, double blooms, very free-flowering. Dark green foliage. Strong, upright and bushy growth. Height 2–2½ft (60–75cm). ❀

Max Jaffa (Burns–UK–1985) Orient-pink sepals. The petals in the corolla are violet, becoming paler at the base, with mandarin-orange edges. Medium, single flowers produced throughout the season. Dark green foliage with red veining. Height 18in (45cm). ❀

Meditation (Blackwell–UK–1956) Red sepals. The petals in the corolla are creamy white, veined with carmine. Small, fluffy, double blooms, produced very early, free-flowering. Upright and bushy growth. Height 15in (38cm). ❀❀

Merlin (Adams–UK–1982) Bright red sepals. The petals in the corolla are deep purple flushed with pink, with pink veining. Small, single flowers with dark green foliage. Tall, upright and self-branching bush. Height 2ft (60cm). ❀❀

***F. microphylla* ssp. *hemsleyana* (*Encliandra specie*)** Both the sepals and the petals in the corolla are red. Tiny, single, solitary flowers produced in the leaf axils. Mid- to dark green foliage. Upright and bushy plants. Very easy to grow. Height 2ft (60cm). ❀❀

(Above) *Merlin.*
F. microphylla *ssp.* hidalgensis.

***F. microphylla* ssp. *hidalgensis* (*Encliandra specie*)** The sepals and the petals in the corolla are both white. Tiny, single, solitary flowers produced in the leaf axils. Very small, dark green foliage. Upright and vigorous growth. Worth using as a bonsai-type specimen. The only totally white species. Height 2ft (60cm). ❀❀

***F. microphylla* ssp. *microphylla* (*Encliandra specie*)** The sepals and the petals in the corolla are both purplish-red. Tiny, single, solitary flowers produced in the leaf axils. Very small leaves. Very bushy growth. Can be used in bonsai-style growth. Height 2ft (60cm). ❀❀

Mischief (Tabraham–UK–1985) Light pink sepals edged rose and tipped with green. The petals in the corolla are mauve with a pink base, maturing to deep pink. Medium, single flowers. Dark green foliage. Compact dwarf bush. Height 9–15in (23–38cm). ❀

Mischief.

Mission Bells (Walker & Jones–USA–1948) Scarlet sepals with rich purple petals in the corolla. Medium to large, single, bell-shaped flowers, very freely produced. Upright and bushy growth. Will make an excellent standard. Height 18in (45cm). ❀

F. microphylla *ssp.* microphylla.

Montrose Village (Richardson–Australia–1985) The sepals are white and the petals in the corolla are spectrum violet and white. Large, round, double flowers. Dark green foliage with lanceolate leaves that are very large with serrated edges. Grows as a lax upright or stiff trailer. Height 18in (45cm). ❀

Monument (Story–UK–1865) Carmine sepals. The petals in the corolla open very dark blue with pinky-carmine petaloids, maturing to pinky-purple with a white base and carmine veining. Large, double flowers. Mid-green foliage with red veining. Height 18in (45cm). ❀❀

(Above) *Mission Bells.*
(Above right) *Monument.*
(Right) *Mr A Huggett.*

Mr A Huggett (Unknown–UK–1930) Scarlet-cerise sepals with mauve-pink petals in the corolla. Smallish, single flowers, produced throughout the summer and into the autumn. Mid-green smallish foliage. Upright and bushy growth. Height 2ft (60cm). BFS showbench hardy. ❀❀

Mrs J D Fredericks.

Mrs Popple.

Mrs J D Fredericks (Evans & Reeves–USA–1936) The sepals, which tend to curl back, are salmon-pink on the upper surface and pale rose on the lower. The petals in the corolla are deep rose, edged with darker rose, with pale orange at the base and an orange vein. Fairly small, single, bell-shaped flowers. Mid-green foliage with red stems. Height 2ft (60cm). ❀❀

Mrs Popple (Elliot–UK–1899) Scarlet sepals. The petals in the corolla are purple-violet veined with cerise. Medium, single flowers, freely produced. Upright, strong and bushy growth. Will make a good hedge. Height 3ft (90cm). BFS show-bench hardy. ❀❀❀❀

Mrs W Castle (Porter–UK–1984) Scarlet sepals. The petals in the corolla are pink-mauve with red veining. Medium, single or semi-double flowers, freely produced. Dark green foliage. Strong, upright growth. Height 3ft (90cm). ❀❀❀

Mrs W Rundle (Rundle–UK–1883) Flesh-pink sepals with rich orange-vermilion petals in the corolla. Large, long, single flowers. Mid- to light green foliage. Growth is as a lax bush or trailer. Will make a fine weeping standard. Height 18in (45cm). ❀

N

Navy Blue (Tabraham–UK–1974) Deep pink sepals with navy blue petals in the corolla. Medium, single flowers, borne in profusion. Pale green foliage. Upright and bushy growth. Height 2ft (60cm). ❀

Neue Welt.

(Below) *Nicola Jane.*

Neue Welt (Mahnke–Germany–1912) Rich red sepals with dark parma-violet petals in the corolla. Small, single blooms, very free-flowering – often producing more than two flowers at each leaf axil. Soft, green foliage with a paler vein. Height 2ft (60cm). BFS showbench hardy. ❀❀

Nicola Jane (Dawson–UK–1959) Cerise-pink sepals. The petals in the corolla are bluish-pink, flushed with cerise. Medium, double flowers, freely produced. Upright and bushy growth. Height 18in (45cm). BFS showbench hardy. ❀

Nunthorpe Gem (Arcadia Nursery–UK–1970) Bright red sepals. The petals in the corolla are deep purple with small, rose-pink petaloids streaked with purple. Medium, double flowers and mid-green foliage. Bushy growth. Height 15in (38cm). ❀❀❀

Nunthorpe Gem.

F. obconica.

O

***F. obconica* (*Ecliandra specie*)** (Breedlove–Mexico–1969) Greenish-white sepals with white petals in the corolla. Tiny, single, solitary flowers produced in the leaf axils. Small, mid-green foliage. Bushy habit. Useful for bonsai work. Height 15in (38cm). ❀❀

P

Papoose (Reedstrom–USA–1960) Bright red sepals with very dark purple petals in the corolla. Small, semi-double flowers are prolifically produced – in fact there are usually more flowers than leaves. Growth is as low bush, versatile for any training – excellent for half standard and makes a wonderful basket. BFS showbench hardy. ❀❀❀

Patricia (Wood–UK–1940) Pale salmon sepals with rosy-cerise petals in the corolla. Small to medium, single flowers, very freely produced. Mid-green foliage. Upright and bushy growth. Height 15in (38cm). ❀

Pee Wee Rose (Niederholzer–USA–1939) Rosy-red sepals. The petals in the corolla are rose-pink edged with rosy-red. Small to medium, single or semi-double flowers, produced in profusion. Small, mid-green foliage. Grows as a rather

(Above) *Papoose.*
(Right) *Pee Wee Rose.*

willowy lax bush. Height 18in (45cm). BFS show-bench hardy. ❀❀

Peggy King (Wood–UK–1954) Rosy-red sepals. The petals in the corolla are paeony-purple, suffused rose, with a carmine vein. Small to medium, single flowers with mid-green foliage. Upright, bushy growth. Height 2½ft (75cm). ❀❀

Peter James (Rolt–UK–1990) Rose sepals, tipped with green. The petals in the corolla are light purplish-pink, heavily veined rose-red, with numerous small petaloids. Medium, semi-double flowers with olive-green foliage. Grows as a willowy bush. Height 18in (45cm). ❀❀

Peter Pan (Unknown) Scarlet, half-open sepals. The petals in the corolla are dark purple maturing

(Above left) *Peggy King.*
(Above) *Pink Lace.*

Pixie.

to fuchsia-purple. Mid-green foliage with red stems. Height 12in (30cm) maximum. ❀❀

Phenomenal (Lemoine–France–1869) Scarlet sepals. The petals in the corolla are rich indigo-blue, paler at the base, with slight carmine veining. Large, heavy, double flowers, fairly freely produced. Upright and bushy growth, needs support to take the weight of the flowers. Height 18in (45cm). ❀❀

Phyllis (Brown–UK–1938) Waxy rose sepals with rose-cerise petals in the corolla. Small to medium, semi-double flowers, very free and early. Yellowish-green foliage. Strong, upright and bushy growth. Ideal for standards and other large structures. Carries many flowers with five sepals. BFS showbench hardy. Height 3–4ft (90-120cm). ❀❀❀

Phyrne (Lemoine–France–1905) Rich cerise sepals. The petals in the corolla are white, heavily veined with cerise. Very large, fully double blooms, freely produced. Dark green, crinkled foliage. Strong, upright and bushy growth. Height 2½ft (75cm). BFS showbench hardy. ❀❀

Pink Goon (Hobson–UK–1982) Red sepals. The petals in the corolla are apple-blossom pink with deeper pink veins. Large, double flowers. Mid-green foliage. Upright and vigorous growth. Height 2ft (60cm). ❀❀

Pink Lace (Tabraham–UK–1974) Red sepals with pink petals in the corolla. Large, double flowers, very freely produced. Mid-green foliage. Strong, upright and bushy growth. Height 2ft (60cm). ❀

Pixie (Russell–UK–1960) Pale cerise sepals. The petals in the corolla are rose-mauve, veined with carmine. Medium flowers, a heavy and continuous bloomer. Yellowish-green foliage with crimson veins. Upright and bushy growth. Height 3ft (90cm). BFS showbench hardy. ❀❀❀

Plenty (Gadsby–UK–1974) Neyron-rose sepals. The petals in the corolla are violet shading to purplish-pink towards the base. Medium, single, bell-shaped flowers, carried in profusion. Mid-green foliage. Strong upright bush. Height 2ft (60cm). ❀❀

Prelude (Blackwell–UK–1957) Red sepals with magenta petals in the corolla. Medium, double flowers, carried in large clusters. Upright and bushy growth. Height 2ft (60cm). ❀❀

Prelude.

President.

President Elliot.

President (Standish–UK–1811) Bright red sepals. The petals in the corolla are reddish-purple with a rose base and heavy scarlet veining. Medium, single flowers. Mid- to dark green foliage turning a distinctive dark red. Strong, upright growth. Height 2ft (60cm). BFS showbench hardy. ❀❀❀

President Elliot (Thorne–UK–1962) Waxy red sepals. The petals in the corolla are reddish-purple with carmine veining. Large, single flowers. Mid- to light green foliage with a red central vein. Strong, upright growth. Height 2ft (60cm). BFS showbench hardy. ❀❀❀

President George Bartlett (Bielby & Oxtoby–UK–1997) Dark cardinal-red sepals. The petals in the corolla open dark violet-purple and mature to rich ruby-red. Medium, semi-double or double flowers with dark foliage. Easy to grow and good in the border or tubs. Height 18in (45cm). ❀❀

President Leo Boullemier (Burns–UK–1983) White sepals streaked with magenta. The petals in the corolla are magenta-blue maturing to blush-pink. Medium, single flowers, perfectly shaped. Dark green foliage. Upright and bushy growth. Height 15in (38cm). ❀

President George Bartlett.

(Below) *Preston Guild.*

Preston Guild (Thornley–UK–1971) Pure white sepals with violet-blue petals in the corolla. Small, single flowers, very freely produced. Mid-green foliage. Upright and bushy growth. Height 18in (45cm). ❀❀

Pride of the West (Lye–UK–1871) Red sepals streaked with paler rose. The petals in the corolla are violet with a pale red base and dark red veins and edges. Medium to large, single flowers. Pale to mid-green foliage. Strong and upright growth. Height 2½ft (90cm). ❀

Prince of Orange (Banks–UK–1872) Waxy salmon-pink sepals. The petals in the corolla are deep salmon-orange. Large, single blooms, early flowering. Fairly soft, upright and bushy growth that needs staking. Height 18in (45cm). ❀

***F. procumbens* (*Procumbetes specie*)** (Cunningham–New Zealand–1834) No petals. The flower has a greenish-yellow tube with green sepals, tipped with purple. Bright blue pollen. Small flowers facing upright from long trailing stems. Small heart-shaped leaves. The prostrate growth can stretch for 3–4ft (1–1.2m). ❀

Prosperity (Gadsby–UK–1970) Waxy crimson sepals. The petals in the corolla are pale neyron-rose, flushed with red. Medium, double flowers, freely produced. Glossy, dark green foliage with large leaves. Upright and bushy growth. Height 2ft (60cm). BFS showbench hardy. ❀❀❀

Purple Splendour (Sunningdale Nurseries–UK–1975) Bright, glossy, crimson sepals. The petals in the corolla are rich blue maturing to blue-mauve. Medium, double flowers with mid-green foliage. Strong, upright growth. Height 2ft (60cm). BFS showbench hardy. ❀❀

Q

Query (Bass–UK–1848) White-edged sepals, blushed with rose. The petals in the corolla are mauvish-violet with a pale rose base. Small to medium, single flowers, profusely produced. Mid- to pale green foliage. Upright and bushy growth. Height 2ft (60cm). ❀❀❀

Prosperity.

Query.

R

Radcliffe Bedder (Roe–UK–1980) Crimson sepals with spectrum-violet petals in the corolla. Medium, semi-double flowers with mid-green foliage. Strong, upright growth. Aptly named – makes a good bedding plant. Height 18–24in (45–60cm). ❀❀

Radings Michelle (*Hybrid* × *F. bacillaris*) (Reimann Merv–The Netherlands–1986) Pink sepals with rose-pink, wavy-edged petals in the corolla. Tiny, single flowers. Small, mid-green foliage produces a spreading bush. Will not tolerate overwatering or drying out in the early stages. Height 18in (45cm). ❀

Red Imp.

Reading Show (Wilson–UK–1967) Red sepals, tipped with green. The petals in the corolla are deep blue-purple and red at the base. Medium, double flowers. Mid- to dark green foliage with red veins. Upright bush. Height 15–18in (38–45cm). BFS showbench hardy. ❀❀

Red Ace (Roe–UK–1983) Bright red sepals. The petals in the corolla are Indian lake. Medium, double flowers, freely produced. Very strong, upright and bushy growth. Height 2ft (60cm). ❀❀

Red Imp (Tabraham–UK–1985) Red sepals with dark purple/wine-red petals in the corolla. Medium, double flowers, continuously produced. Dark purple/green foliage. Dwarf upright and bushy growth. Height 9–15in (23–38cm). ❀

***F. regia* (*Quelusia specie*)** Red sepals with purple petals in the corolla. Smallish, single flowers. The mid-green leaves have pronounced red veins. Strong but lax growth. Bush or shrub training. Height 2½ft (75cm), spread 2–3ft (60–90cm). ❀❀❀

***F. regia* ssp. *regia* (*Quelusia specie*)** (Vandelli–Brazil–1943) Red sepals with purple petals in the corolla. Smallish, single flowers. Mid-green foliage. Very vigorous growth capable of achieving 20ft (6m) in a good growing year. Needs to be trained as a climber – *not* suitable for containing within pots. ❀❀❀

***F. regia* ssp. *reitzii* (*Quelusia specie*)** (Berry–Brazil–1959) Red sepals with purple petals in the corolla. Small, single, solitary or paired flowers. Mid-green foliage. Very vigorous growth with branches reaching 10–12ft (3–3.6m) forming a large bush. ❀❀❀

***F. regia* ssp. *serrae* (*Quelusia specie*)** (Berry–Brazil–1985) Red sepals with purple petals in the corolla. Small to medium, single, solitary flowers. Mid-green foliage. Very vigorous, sprawling growth. A climbing shrub in its natural habitat. ❀❀❀

Remembrance (Gubler–UK–1995) Rose-red sepals. The petals in the corolla are pale purplish-pink with rose-red veining. Medium, semi-double

Richard John Carrington.

(Below) *Robin Hood.*

flowers, very prolific. Mid-green foliage. Strong, upright and bushy growth. A 'sport' of 'Margaret'. Height 3–4ft (90–120cm). ❀❀❀

Richard John Carrington (Unknown) Bright cerise sepals that curl back, twisting slightly. The petals in the corolla are blue-violet with cerise veining. Medium, single flowers. Young foliage is light green maturing to dark green. Upright, bushy growth. Height 18in (45cm). ❀❀

Robin Hood (Colville–UK–1966) Bright red/cerise sepals with green tips. The petals in the corolla open deep violet, overlaid and splashed with cerise, maturing to a deep plum colour. Very large, double flowers. Mid-green foliage on an upright bush. Height 18in (45cm). ❀❀

Rose of Castille (Banks–UK–1855) Waxy white sepals, tipped with green. The petals in the corolla are purple, faintly flushed with rose, with a white base. Small to medium, single flowers with mid-green foliage. Upright, bushy growth. Height 18in (45cm). BFS showbench hardy. ❀❀

Rose of Castille Improved (Banks–UK–1869) Flesh-pink sepals with violet-purple petals in the corolla. Medium, single flowers, freely produced. Lightish green foliage. Upright, vigorous and bushy growth. Height 2½ft (75cm). BFS showbench hardy. ❀❀

Rose of Denmark (Banks–UK–1864) The sepals are white, blushed pink. The petals in the corolla

Rose of Castille.

(Below) *Rose of Castille Improved.*

(Above) *Rose of Denmark.*

open pale rose-lavender maturing to rose-pink, with a whitish base and pink veins. Medium, single flowers, very freely produced. Mid-green foliage, lighter underneath. Lax growth. Height 18in (45cm). ❀

Rose Lea (Griffiths–UK–1978) Deep cerise sepals. The petals in the corolla are royal purple with a dusky-rose base. One petal between each sepal is dusky pink with a purple splash. Small but numerous double flowers. Mid-green foliage with red stems. Medium, bushy growth. Height 15in (38cm). ❀❀

Royal Purple (Lemoine–France–*c.*1896) Deep cerise sepals. The petals in the corolla are rich purple with red veins, becoming lighter at the base. Large, semi-double blooms, free-flowering. Upright and bushy – will make a fine standard. Height 18in (45cm). ❀❀

Rufus (Nelson–USA–1952) The sepals and the petals in the corolla are both bright turkey-red (self coloured). Medium, single flowers, very free-flowering. Upright, strong and bushy growth – will make a fine standard. Height 18in (45cm). BFS showbench hardy. ❀❀

Ruth (Wood–UK–1949) Rose-red sepals with purplish-red petals in the corolla. Medium, single

Rose Lea.

blooms, very free-flowering. Mid-green foliage. Upright and bushy growth. Height 18in (45cm). BFS showbench hardy. ❀❀❀

S

Santa Cruz (Tiret–USA–1947) The sepals and the petals in the corolla are both deep crimson. Largish, semi-double flowers, freely produced. Large, mid-green foliage with red veining. Upright and bushy growth. Height 2ft (60cm). BFS showbench hardy. ❀❀

Sarah Jane (Putley–UK–1974) Red sepals. The petals in the corolla are lilac splashed with rose, with a dark lilac base and veins. Small to medium rosette-like double flowers. Mid-green foliage. Upright and bushy growth. Height 15in (38cm). ❀

(Left) *Rufus.*
(Below) *Ruth.*

(Above left) *Santa Cruz.*
(Above) *Sarah Jane.*

Scarcity.

Schneeball.

(Below) *Sealand Prince.*

Saturnus (de Groot–The Netherlands–1970) Bright crimson sepals. The petals in the corolla are imperial-purple shading to phlox-purple with red veining. Smallish, single flowers with mid-green foliage. Small upright bush. Height 12–15in (30–38cm). ❀

Scarcity (Lye–UK–1869) Cerise sepals. The petals in the corolla open purple with fine, deep red edges and red veins, maturing to reddish purple with a rose base. Medium, single flowers with mid- to light green foliage. Height 18in (45cm). ❀❀❀

Schneeball (Klein–Germany–1874) Bright pink sepals. The petals in the corolla are white, veined pink or red. Small, semi-double, ball-shaped flowers, freely produced. Light green foliage. Upright and bushy growth. Height 15in (38cm). ❀❀

Schneewitchen (Klein–Germany–1878) Bright red sepals with dark red markings towards the tips. The petals in the corolla are white with red veining. Medium, semi-double flowers. Dark green foliage with deep red central veins. Upright, bushy growth. Very similar to 'Snowcap'. Height 18in (45cm). ❀

Schneewitcher (Hoech–Germany–1884) Rich, waxy, red sepals. The petals in the corolla are rich violet-blue. Medium, single, wide-open blooms, free-flowering. Upright and bushy growth. Height 18in (45cm). BFS showbench hardy. ❀❀

Sealand Prince (Walker Bees Nurseries–UK–1967) Light red sepals with violet-purple petals in the corolla. Medium, single blooms, free-flowering. Mid-green foliage. Grows as an open and upright bush. Height 2½ft (75cm). ❀

Silverpink.

Sleepy.

Sharon Caunt (Caunt–UK–1987) Rose-madder sepals. The petals in the corolla are white, veined with rose-madder. Medium, fully-double flowers with mid-green foliage. Upright and bushy growth. Height 18in (45cm). ❀❀

Silverdale (Travis–UK–1962) Eau-de-nil sepals with pastel-lavender petals in the corolla. Small, single, barrel-shaped flowers, very freely produced. Small, pale green foliage. Upright and bushy growth. Height 18in (45cm). BFS showbench hardy. ❀

Silverpink (Tabraham–UK–1978) Single. Tube and sepals deep pink. Corolla silver pink – half flared. Medium-sized flowers produced in mid-season. Mid-green foliage. Growth upright and bushy, but can sprawl. Height to about 18in (45cm) with a spread of 2ft (60cm).

Sleepy (Tabraham–UK–1954) Pale pink sepals with lavender-blue petals in the corolla. Small, single flowers, continuously produced. Pale green foliage. Upright and bushy growth – dwarf habit. Height 9–15in (23–38cm). BFS showbench hardy. ❀

Sneezy (Tabraham–UK–1974) Red sepals with deep lavender-blue petals in the corolla. Small, single flowers, very freely produced. Light green foliage. Upright and bushy growth – very dainty. Dwarf habit. Height 9–15in (23–38cm). BFS showbench hardy. ❀

Snowcap (Henderson–UK–1880) Bright red sepals. The petals in the corolla are white, veined with cerise. Small to medium, semi-double flowers, very profuse. Mid-green foliage. Upright and vigorous growth. Will make a superb standard. Height 2ft (60cm). BFS showbench hardy. ❀❀

Son of Thumb (Gubler–UK–1978) Cerise sepals with lilac petals in the corolla. Small, semi-double flowers, very prolific. A 'sport' of 'Tom Thumb' with growth and habit identical to its parent. Height 15in (38cm). BFS showbench hardy. ❀❀❀

Strawberry Supreme (Gadsby–UK–1970) Waxy bright crimson sepals. The petals in the corolla are dull white heavily veined and base carmine-rose. Medium to large, double flowers. Yellowish-green foliage with slight bronzing, red veins and stems. Upright, bushy growth. Height 18in (45cm). ❀❀

Susan Green (Caunt–UK–1981) White to pale pink with pale green tips, the sepals curve upright and slightly twist. The petals in the corolla are rose-pink with a thin edge of dark rose. Medium, single, funnel-shaped flowers. Pale to mid-green foliage. Height 15in (38cm). ❀

Susan Travis (Travis–UK–1958) Deep pink sepals. The petals in the corolla are rose-pink with a paler base. Medium, single flowers, very prolific. Mid-green foliage. Vigorous, spreading bush. Height 2ft (60cm). BFS showbench hardy. ❀❀

T

Tennessee Waltz (Walker & Jones–USA–1951) Rose-madder sepals with petals coloured with lilac, rose and lavender in the corolla. Medium, semi-double flowers borne continuously through the summer. Mid-green foliage. Upright, strong growth. Makes a good standard. Height 2ft (60cm). BFS showbench hardy. ❀❀

The Doctor (Castle Nurseries–UK) Flesh-pink sepals with rose-salmon petals in the corolla. Medium, single flowers. Mid-green, rounded foliage. Soft, lax growth – will need support to make a bush and is probably best as a weeping standard or in a hanging container – excellent for the edge of a window box. Height 18in (45cm). ❀

The Tarns (Travis–UK–1962) Pale pink sepals with a rose reverse. The petals in the corolla are violet-blue shading to rose at the base. Medium, single flowers, very freely produced. Dark green foliage. Upright, bushy habit. Height 2ft (60cm). BFS showbench hardy. ❀❀❀

Therese Dupuis (Lemoine–France) Crimson sepals with reddish-purple petals in the corolla. Large, single flowers. Mid- to dark green foliage. Strong, upright growth. Height 3ft (90cm). ❀❀

Thornley's Hardy (Thornley–UK–1970) Waxy white sepals with red petals in the corolla. Smallish, single flowers, very freely produced. Growth is

Therese Dupuis.

as lax bush or trailer. Height 12in (30cm), spread 18in (45cm). BFS showbench hardy. ❀

Tinkerbell (Tabraham–UK–1976) Red sepals with white petals in the corolla. Small, single, bell-shaped flowers, very profuse. Dark green foliage. Dwarf upright bush. Height 9–12in (23–30cm). ❀

Tom Thumb (Baudinot–France–1850) Carmine sepals. The petals in the corolla are mauve, veined with carmine. Small, single flowers are produced in profusion throughout the summer. Upright growth – very suitable for rockeries or the front of a hardy border. Height 15in (38cm). BFS showbench hardy. ❀❀❀

Tom West (Miellez–France–1853) The sepals are rich carmine. The petals in the corolla are purple. Medium, single blooms, free-flowering. Variegated foliage of green, cream and cerise. Upright, bushy growth. As it is usually grown for its foliage and continuously pinched to get the best colour of foliage, the flowers are not often seen at their best. Height 18in (45cm). ❀❀

Tracid (Colville–UK–1980) Red sepals. The petals in the corolla are pale pink with deep pink veins and base. Medium, semi-double flowers. Mid-green foliage. Strong, upright bush. Height 18in (45cm). ❀❀

Trase (Dawson–UK–1959) Carmine-cerise sepals. The petals in the corolla are white, veined and flushed carmine-cerise. Medium, semi-double flowers, very freely produced. Upright and bushy growth. Height 18in (45cm). BFS showbench hardy. ❀❀❀

Trudy (Gadsby–UK–1969) The sepals are white, edged with pink, with pale green tips on the upper

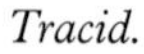

Tracid.

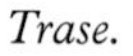

Trase.

Vielliebchen.

surface and rhodamine-pink on the lower. The sepals curl back. The petals in the corolla are violet-blue with a rhodamine base and red veining. Small, single, bell-shaped flowers. Mid-green foliage. Bushy growth. Height 18in (45cm). ❀❀

V

Venus Victrix (Gulliver–UK–1840) The sepals are white, tinged with green. The petals in the corolla are violet-purple, shading to white at the base. Very small, single flowers. Mid-green foliage. Upright bush. Can be very difficult. 'Venus Victrix' was a benchmark in the history of fuchsias being the first cultivar to have white tubes and sepals. Height 12–15in (30–38cm). ❀❀

Vielliebchen (Wolf–Germany–1911) The sepals are red with a glossy red tube. The petals in the corolla are deep purple, maturing to red-purple. Small, single flowers, prolific. Mid-green foliage. Upright bush. Height 12in (30cm). ❀❀❀

Violet Lace (Tabraham–UK–1982) Red sepals. The petals in the corolla are violet, splashed with pink. Large, double blooms, free-flowering. Mid-green foliage. A solid, upright bush. Height 18–24in (45–60cm). ❀

Voltaire (Lemoine–France–1897) Scarlet sepals. The petals in the corolla are magenta with scarlet veining. Medium, single flowers. Mid-green foliage. Strong, upright growth. Height 2ft (60cm). BFS showbench hardy. ❀❀

W

Wagtails White Pixie (Unknown) Carmine red sepals. The petals in the corolla are white and veined with carmine. Small, single flowers (like a

Voltaire.

(Above left) *White Clove.*
(Above) *Whiteknight's Amethyst.*

Whiteknight's Blush.

Whiteknight's Green Glister.

miniature 'Snowcap'). Light to mid-green foliage shading to darker green at the tips, with red veins and stems. Height 12in (30cm). ❀❀❀

Waldfee (*Hybrid F.* × *bacillaris*) (Travis–UK–1973) Lilac-pink self (sepals and petals in the corolla are all lilac-pink). Very small, single flowers. Matt, forest-green, small foliage. Tall and bushy growth. Can be encouraged to trail. Height 3ft (90cm). ❀❀

Wharfdale (Unknown) The sepals are of the palest pink and curl back. The petals in the corolla are purplish-rose with pale bases and veins, and fine orange edging. Medium, single flowers. Mid-green foliage. Height 18in (45cm). ❀❀

White Clove (*Hybrid F.* × *bacillaris*) (Unknown) The tube is white. Purple sepals with mauvish-pink petals in the corolla. Single blooms, one of the tiniest of flowers. Mid-green, fern-like foliage. Height 2ft (60cm). ❀❀

Whiteknight's Amethyst (Wright–UK–1980) The sepals are deep purplish-pink, with green tips. The petals in the corolla are dark reddish-purple. Smallish, single flowers. Dark green foliage. Strong growth – will produce strong basal shoots each spring. Height 2ft (60cm) plus. BFS showbench hardy. ❀❀❀

Whiteknight's Blush (Wright–UK–1980) The sepals and the petals in the corolla are both pale pink. Small, single flowers very similar to 'Whiteknight's Pearl' but the growth is lower and more spreading. Height and width approximately 2ft (60cm). BFS showbench hardy. ❀❀❀

Whiteknight's Green Glister (Wright–UK–1980) Light red sepals, paling towards the edges. The petals in the corolla are reddish-purple with light red edges and base. Small, single flowers. Mid-green foliage. Needs staking to maintain a 2ft (60cm) bush. BFS showbench hardy. ❀❀❀

Whiteknight's Pearl (Wright–UK–1980) Pale pink sepals with clear pink petals in the corolla. Smallish, single flowers enhanced by the small, dark green foliage. Medium upright growth. Height 3ft (90cm) plus. BFS showbench hardy. ❀❀❀

White Pixie (Merrist Wood–UK–1968) Rich carmine sepals. The petals in the corolla are white, veined with pink. Smallish, single flowers, very freely produced. Yellowish-green foliage with crimson veins. Upright and bushy growth. Height 3ft (90cm). BFS showbench hardy. ❀❀❀

Wicked Queen (Tabraham–UK–1985) Dark red sepals. The petals in the corolla are deep purple, splashed with pink. Very large, double flowers. Very dark green foliage. Upright, bushy and compact growth. Height 2ft (60cm). ❀

Woodside (Dawson–UK–1985) Rosy-red sepals with mid-lilac petals in the corolla. Very large, fully double blooms, can be rather late in flowering. Dark green foliage. Upright and bushy growth. Height 18in (45cm). ❀

W P Wood (Wood–UK–1954) Scarlet sepals. The petals in the corolla are violet-blue with scarlet bases and heavy veining. Medium, single blooms can be late in flowering. Darkish green foliage on an upright bush. Height 2ft (60cm). BFS showbench hardy. ❀❀

(Above) *Whiteknight's Pearl.*

Wicked Queen.

CHAPTER 13

Specialist Fuchsia Nurseries

Please remember to include two or three first class stamps when requesting copies of catalogues.

Alderton Plant Nursery
Pam Hutchinson, Spring Lane, Alderton, Towcester, Northamptonshire NN12 7LW. Tel: 01327 811253. *No postal service*

Arcadia Nurseries
Brass Castle Lane, Nunthorpe, Middlesborough, Cleveland TS8 9EB. Tel: 01642 300817. *Postal service*

Askew Nurseries
South Croxton Road, Queniborough, Leicester LE7 3RX. Tel: 01664 840557. *Postal service*

B & H M Baker
Bourne Brook Nurseries, Greenstead Green, Halstead, Essex CO9 1RJ. Tel: 01787 472900. *No postal service*

Bellcross Nurseries
Howden, Goole, East Yorkshire DN14 7TQ. Tel: 01430 430284. *No postal service*

Blackwell Fuchsia Nursery
Woodbine Cottage, Blackwell, Near Shipston-on-Stour, Warwickshire CV36 4PE. Tel: 01608 682531. *Postal service*

Breach Lane Nursery
Breach Lane, Wootton Bassett, Swindon, Wiltshire SN4 7QR. Tel: 01793 854660. *No postal service*

Brigadoon Fuchsias
25 King's Way, Lyme Regis, Dorset DT7 3DU. Tel: 01297 445566. *Postal service only*

Brynawel Garden Centre (Fisher Fuchsias)
Sully Road, Penarth, Vale of Glamorgan CF64 3UU.
Tel: 01222 702660. *Postal service*

Breach Lane Nursery, Swindon.

Burnside Fuchsias
Parsonage Road, Blackburn, Lancashire
BB1 4AG. Tel: 01254 249203. *Postal service*

Chase Fuchsias
Pye Green Road, Hednesfield, Cannock,
Staffordshire WS12 4LP. Tel: 01543 422394.
Postal service

Clay Lane Nursery
Ken Belton, 3 Clay Lane, South Nutfield, Near
Redhill, Surrey RH1 4EG. Tel: 01737 823307.
No postal service

Clifton Plant Centre
Clifton, Morpeth, Northumberland NE61 6DG.
Tel: 01670 515024. *Postal service*

Exotic Fuchsias
Pen-y-banc Nurseries, Crwbin, Kidwelly,
Carmarthenshire SA17 5DP. Tel: 01269 870729.
Postal service

Fenland Fuchsias
Cyril & Jenny Waters, Old Main Road, Fleet
Hargate, Spalding, Lincolnshire PE12 8LL.
Tel: 01406 423709. *No postal service*

Fine Fuchsias (David Fox, Nurseryman)
34 Cottrell Road, Eastville, Bristol BS5 6TJ.
Tel: 0117 951 8819. *Postal service*

Fuchsiavale Nurseries
John Ridding, Worcester Road, Torton,
Kidderminster, Worcestershire DY11 7SB.
Tel: 01299 251162. *Limited postal service*

Clay Lane Nursery, Redhill.

Fuchsiaworld Plant Centre
Cedar Nursery, Birdham Road, Chichester, West Sussex PO20 7EQ. Tel: 01243 776822. *Postal service*

Glenacres Nursery
Wimborne Road West, Stapehill, Wimborne, Dorset BH21 2DY. Tel: 01202 872069. *Postal wholesale service*

Gouldings Fuchsias
Link Lane, Bentley, Near Ipswich, Suffolk IP9 2DP. Tel: 01473 310058. *Postal service*

Island Garden Nursery
Church Street, Upwey, Weymouth, Dorset DT3 5QB. Tel: 01305 814345. *Mail order enquiries* – Beacon Fuchsias, 32 Markham Avenue, Bournemouth BH10 7HN

Jackson's Nurseries
Clifton Campville, Near Tamworth, Staffordshire B79 0AP. Tel: 01827 373307. *No mail order*

Kathleen Muncaster Fuchsias
18 Field Lane, Morton, Gainsborough, Lincolnshire DN21 3BY. Tel: 01427 612329. *Limited postal service*

Little Brook Fuchsias
Carol Gubler, Little Brook, Ash Green Lane West, Ash Green, Near Aldershot, Hampshire GU12 6HL. Tel: 01252 329731. *No postal service*

Littleton Nursery
Littleton, Near Somerton, Somerset TA11 6NT. Tel: 01458 272356. *Postal service*

C S Lockyer (Fuchsias)
70 Henfield Road, Coalpit Heath, Bristol BS17 2UZ. Tel: 01454 772219. *Postal service*

Mike Oxtoby Fuchsias
74 Westgate, North Cave, Brough, East Yorkshire HU15 2NJ. Tel: 01430 423049. *Postal Service*

Oakleigh Nurseries
Petersfield Road, Monkswood, Alresford, Hampshire SO24 0HB. Tel: 01962 773344. *Postal service*

Oldbury Nurseries
Brissenden Green, Betersden, Ashford, Kent TN26 3BJ. Tel: 01233 820416. *Postal service*

Oli-Bee Nursery
Pegmire Lane, Aldenham, Watford, Hertfordshire WD2 8DR. Tel: 01923 853117. *Postal service*

Percival's Fuchsias
Hill Farm, Bures Road, White Colne, Colchester, Essex CO6 2QA. Tel: 01787 222541. *Postal service*

Potash Nursery
Mike Clare, The Cottage, Cow Green, Near Stowmarket, Suffolk IP14 4HJ. Tel: 01449 781671. *Limited postal service*

Riverside Fuchsias
Puddefoot, Gravel Road, Sutton at Hone, Dartford, Kent DA4 9HQ. Tel: 01322 863891. *Postal service*

Rookery Farm Nursery
5 Rookery Road, Wyboston, Bedfordshire MK44 3AX. Tel: 01480 213506. *Postal service*

Rooster Fuchsias
Margaret Bird, 7 Accommodation Road, Boxted, Colchester, Essex CO4 5HR. Tel: 01206 272232. *No postal service*

Roualeyn Fuchsias
'Roualeyn', Trefriw, Conwy, North Wales LL27 0SX. Tel: 01492 640548. *Postal service*

Silver Dale Nurseries
Shute Lane, Combe Martin, North Devon EX34 0HT. Tel: 01271 882539. *Postal service*

John Smith and Son, The Fuchsia Centre
Thornton Nurseries, Thornton, Leicestershire LE67 1AN. Tel: 01530 230331. *Postal service*

St Margaret's Fuchsia Nursery
St Margaret's Lane, Titchfield, Fareham, Hampshire PO14 4BG. Tel: 01329 846006. *No postal service*

Vernon Geranium Nursery
Cuddington Way, Cheam, Surrey SM2 7JB. Tel: 0181 393 7616. *Postal service*

Walton Nurseries (Fuchsia Specialist)
54 Burford Lane, Lymm, Warrington, Cheshire WA13 0SH. Tel: 01925 759026. *Postal service*

Ward Fuchsias
5 Pollen Close, Sale, Manchester M33 3LS. Tel: 0161 282 7434. *Postal service*

Warrenorth Fuchsias
Peter & Marian Simmons, East Grinstead Road, North Chailey, Lewes, East Sussex BN8 4JD. Tel: 01825 723266. *Postal service*

Wayside Fuchsias
Chester Road, Acton, Nantwich, Cheshire CW5 8LB. Tel: 01270 625795. *Postal service*

Wheeler A D & N
Pye Court, Willoughby, Rugby CV23 8BZ. Tel: 01788 890341. *No postal service*

White Veil Fuchsias
Verwood Road, Three Legged Cross, Wimborne, Dorset BH21 6RP. Tel: 01202 813998. *Postal service*

Index

Page numbers in *italic* refer to illustrations.